USNA

THE UNITED STATES NAVAL ACADEMY

Photographs by **Keith Jenkins, Anthony Edgeworth,** and others

USNA

THE UNITED STATES NAVAL ACADEMY

A PICTORIAL CELEBRATION OF 150 YEARS

by Gale Gibson Kohlhagen and Ellen Boraz Heinbach

Editor: Robert Morton
Designer: Liz Trovato

Library of Congress Cataloging-in-
Publication Data

Kohlhagen, Gale Gibson.
    United States Naval Academy: a
pictorial celebration of 150 years / by
Gale Gibson Kohlhagen and Ellen
Boraz Heinbach.
        p.   cm.
    Includes bibliographical references
and index.
    ISBN 0–8109–3932–0
    1. United States Naval Academy—
Pictorial works.   2. United States
Naval Academy—History.   I.
Heinbach, Ellen Boraz.   II. Title.
V415.L3K64   1995
359′.0071′173—dc20   94–25955
                            CIP

Published in 1995 by Harry N. Abrams,
Incorporated, New York
A Times Mirror Company

Printed and bound in Japan

To our families—
Steven, Tron, Kristoff, and Spenser;
Harvey, Michael, Sarah, and
Bud—who would have pitched
pennies at Tecumseh, hopped on
Herndon and rubbed Rickover's nose
if such gestures would have hastened
the completion of our book.

And to Steven,
whose editing helped keep us on
course.

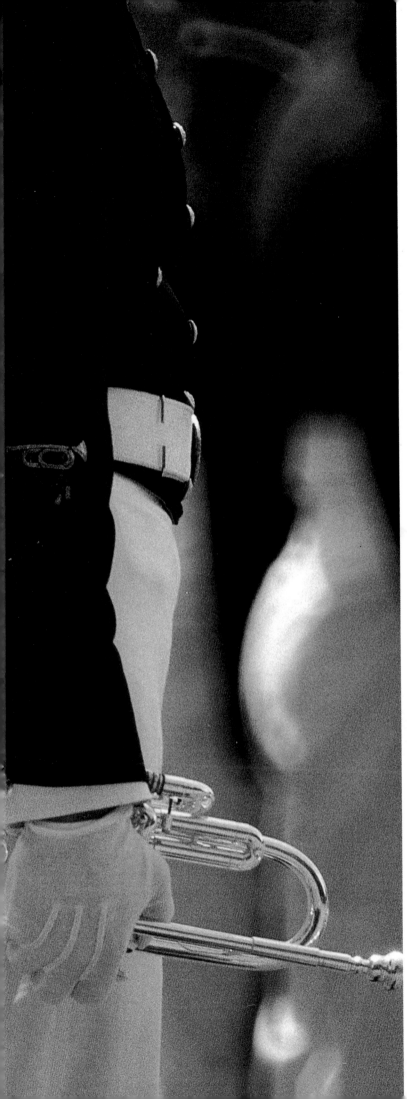

CONTENTS

ACKNOWLEDGMENTS

We owe a great debt to many people in the naval community whose wisdom and enthusiasm for our project have made this book possible. Admirals Kinnaird R. McKee and Thomas H. Moorer; Vice Admirals James F. Calvert, William P. Lawrence, William P. Mack, and Charles S. Minter, Jr.; and Rear Admiral James A. Winnefeld graciously gave of their time, discussing the Academy from their varied perspectives as former superintendents and commandants. Not only did they share their expertise; they also recounted stories of their midshipman days and the lifelong benefits of Academy training.

At the Academy, Superintendent Rear Admiral Thomas C. Lynch met with us and generously offered us access to the rich resources of the school. Rear Admiral Anthony J. Watson, Deputy Commandant, and his successor, Colonel Terrence P. Murray, explained the day-to-day workings of the brigade of midshipmen and allowed us behind the scenes in Bancroft Hall. In addition, Colonel Murray talked with us about the Marine Corps presence at the Academy. Vice Academic Dean William B. Garrett made numerous suggestions and sent us materials to further our research. Athletic Director Jack Lengyel helped us understand the crucial role of Academy athletics and introduced us to Sports Information Director Tom Bates, whose wealth of knowledge and vast store of information on Navy sports proved invaluable.

We could not have succeeded without the help and guidance of the many wonderful people at the Naval Academy Archives, Nimitz Library, the Naval Academy Museum, and the Naval Academy Photo Lab. Kenneth J. Hagan, Archivist and Museum Director, and Jane H. Price, Assistant Archivist; Alice S. Creighton, Assistant Librarian, Special Collections; and James W. Cheevers, Museum Curator, directed our research, identified sources, and enthusiastically supported our work. Their great love for the Academy and their many years of service enabled them to offer insightful advice and assistance. David Eckard, Wayne McCrea, and Ken Mierzejewski gave us access to their photo archives, and a number of their outstanding photographs appear in the book. Paul Stillwell, Director of History at the Naval Institute, guided us through the oral histories of Academy graduates and again and again kept us in mind whenever he came across material relevant to our work.

Many graduates spent hours sharing their memories and giving us the opportunity to understand the Academy at different periods in its history. They conveyed to us the importance of Academy training both in the fleet and in civilian careers. Special thanks go to Captain John L. Prehn, Jr., and

Moonlight bathes the magnificent Naval Academy Chapel—the Cathedral of the Navy.

13

his wife, Mary, who related wonderful stories of the Academy and of the town of Annapolis, allowed us to borrow extensively from their *Lucky Bag* collection, and, most important, provided us with a home away from home on our numerous visits.

Without the unfailing support of the Public Affairs Office, this book could not have been written. Commander Mike John, Public Affairs Officer, and Noel Milan, Director of Academy Relations, met with us frequently, escorted us to Academy events, and dealt with our endless requests with grace and good humor. Debbie Carroll arranged numerous meetings, tours of behind-the-scenes sights, and interviews with midshipmen. She tracked down the most obscure details and was always willing to help us at a moment's notice.

And, of course, we are particularly grateful to all the midshipmen who let us in on the challenges, hardships, and joys of life at the Naval Academy. Despite the thousands of demands on their time, they took us to meals in King Hall, met with us in informal groups, corresponded with us, and entrusted us with their personal experiences and insights.

Within a few hours of their arrival at the Academy, plebes form up in the colonnade connecting Bancroft and Dahlgren halls. As they march to Tecumseh Court to take the oath of office, they begin "the longest year of their lives."

The brigade of midshipmen is divided into two regiments, six battalions, and thirty-six companies. Here, three companies march to the parade field for the Dedication Parade during Commissioning Week.

INTRODUCTION

This excellent book confirms that Secretary of the Navy George Bancroft made a wise decision when he established the U.S. Naval Academy in 1845. Since that time, graduates of the Academy have proudly fulfilled the mission of their school:

"To develop Midshipmen morally, mentally, and physically and to imbue them with the highest ideals of duty, honor, and loyalty in order to provide graduates who are dedicated to a career of naval service and have potential for future development in mind and character to assume the highest responsibilities of command, citizenship, and government."

Most importantly, Academy graduates have steadfastly protected the security of our great nation. They are renowned for their acts of courage in times of war and crisis. Seventy-three graduates have received the Medal of Honor, our country's highest award for valor, and thousands more have been decorated for bravery in action. They have remained unfailingly obedient to civilian authority, a key principal in our constitutional democracy.

In addition to skillfully tracing the rich history of the Academy, the authors very effectively describe the intensive whole-person development process, essential to the molding of military leaders. They explain the Academy's professional programs, in which Midshipmen engage in military drills, learn naval tactics, enhance their leadership skills, and train during the summer with the fleet in Navy ships all around the globe. They provide an excellent understanding of the Academy's superb academic program, comparable to the finest baccalaureate degree programs in the country.

Competitive athletics are an important part of the Midshipmen's daily activity in developing their physical fitness, courage, will to win, and sense of teamwork—vital in the military profession. The authors discuss the proud history of Naval Academy sports, which have consistently produced top teams and individual performers in the country.

Certainly producing the finest naval leaders is the Academy's preeminent purpose, but history has shown that the rigorous selection and training program of the Academy creates genuine national assets. As the authors note, the Academy is the prime supplier of astronauts, naval test pilots, and nuclear engineers, as well as listing many outstanding statesmen, public servants, and business leaders among its graduates.

George Bancroft probably did not fully realize at the time the wisdom of placing the Academy in the historic city of Annapolis, which appears today much as it did in colonial times with more than two hundred buildings over two centuries old. The charming ambience of this quaint city, contiguous to the Academy, makes it an ideal location for an undergraduate school. Since 1845 the citizens of Annapolis have had a love affair with Midshipmen, welcoming them into their homes and serving as their surrogate parents.

The authors have done a splendid job of capturing the true essence of Academy life and conveying a clear sense of its traditions, values, and spirit. But the major contribution of the book is enabling its readers to understand and appreciate the immensely challenging task of preparing young persons to fulfill in the military profession the noblest obligation that can be vested in a citizen—the protection of the nations's freedoms and way of life.

Vice Admiral William P. Lawrence, USN (Ret.)
U.S. Naval Academy Class of 1951 and
Superintendent of the Naval Academy, 1978–1981

After hours of struggle, a plebe finally makes it to the top of the Herndon Monument, which has been greased with lard. As he replaces the hated dixie cup with a midshipman's hat, a cheer goes up, "No more plebes!"

THE ACADEMY AT 150

The whaling trade was thriving; the first propeller-driven steamship crossed the Atlantic; and the potato famine began in Ireland. Texas and Florida were admitted to the Union as slave states; James Polk was inaugurated as president; and Andrew Jackson died. Edgar Allan Poe published "The Raven," and in Annapolis, Maryland, the Naval School was founded at Fort Severn. The year was 1845.

On the morning of October 10 at eleven o'clock, fifty or so young men, seasoned sailors and novices alike, gathered to hear Superintendent Franklin Buchanan set forth his ambitious ideals for the new school. Looking out over the collection of run-down buildings of old Fort Severn, few could imagine that the school would become acclaimed throughout the world as the premier institution for training naval officers. Of those who entered the school that first fall, most were midshipmen who had served at sea as apprentice officers. Although over the years, students at the Academy have been called midshipmen, acting midshipmen, cadet midshipmen, cadet engineers, naval cadets, and, since 1902, midshipmen again, the Academy's goal for them has always been the same: to develop them morally, mentally, and physically as they prepare to assume the highest responsibilities of command in the fleet.

Modern academic halls, designed to harmonize with the Academy's turn-of-the century Beaux-Arts buildings, feature state-of-the-art laboratories and facilities.

During its first fifty years, the Academy became firmly established, and the number of midshipmen entering its gates increased dramatically. Although new buildings were constructed to accommodate them, it was clear by the turn of the century that the facilities were totally inadequate. It fell to wealthy industrialist Robert Means Thompson (Class of 1868) to remedy the situation. As a member of the Board of Visitors in 1895, he reported on the deplorable conditions of the school's buildings and the disgraceful state of the sanitary system. He had the vision to commission prominent New York architect Ernest Flagg to draw up a comprehensive, unified design for the Academy. Flagg's master plan, paid for from Thompson's own funds, insured that construction would no longer proceed in the piecemeal, haphazard fashion of the past. With Thompson's active support, a one-million-dollar appropriation was passed by Congress in 1898, and the rebuilding of the Academy began.

Throughout the Yard—the Academy grounds—stately new Beaux-Arts buildings arose, symbols of the country's faith in the promise of the new century and the Navy's role in demonstrating America's status as a world power. With its majestic rotunda, the imposing new dormitory, Bancroft Hall, became the center of midshipman life. Graceful colonnades connected Bancroft to the Boat House and the Armory. The domed Chapel looked

out on tree-lined walks and down toward the blue waters of the Severn.

Today, as the Academy celebrates its one hundred and fiftieth anniversary, it is clear that Flagg's plan endures. Although new land has been acquired, new buildings have been constructed, and the brigade has increased almost tenfold in number, the Academy has remained true to Thompson's vision at the turn of the century. Stately buildings named for naval greats of the past inspire those who study and prepare for the leadership of tomorrow. "The atmosphere seems to breathe of the great heroes of our Navy—heroes of the days long before the school was founded; heroes of the ensuing years, and heroes of today." The history and traditions of the past, embodied in the monuments and buildings of the Yard, are daily reminders to midshipmen of the heights to which they may aspire.

Over 58,000 midshipmen have been graduated from the Academy. Today, the brigade is four thousand strong, with women accounting for 10 percent of the total. Minorities make up 17 percent, and about four hundred midshipmen have had previous experience in the enlisted ranks of the Navy and the Marine Corps. Midshipmen hail from every state in the nation, from American territories, and from friendly foreign countries. Their reasons for coming are as varied as their backgrounds. For some, there is a family tradition of military service. For others, there is the attraction of an exciting naval career. But for all, there is the dedication to their country's service and the chance to test themselves against the rigorous standards of Academy life.

In their four years together by the Bay, midshipmen face many challenges. From the unrelenting regimentation of plebe year through the progressive assumption of leadership roles, midshipmen gain professional competence and confidence in their own abilities. Through athletics, they develop strength, discipline, and endurance and learn the value of teamwork, which will stand them in good stead in their naval careers. The exacting academic curriculum, with its emphasis on science and engineering, provides both a comprehensive background for junior officers as they take their places in the fleet and a strong foundation for future specialization.

Moral development is a key component of the program. The Honor Concept demands personal integrity "by requiring the midshipmen to live in an environment in which performance of one's duty and adherence to the highest standards of honorable conduct represent the only acceptable way of life." Realizing that under battle conditions the smallest detail may mean the difference between life and death, the Academy holds midshipmen accountable for their every action. Because opportunity and obligation go together,

Even Buchanan House, the stately residence of Academy superintendents since 1906, sports banners and slogans during Army Week.

Above, right: King Hall reverberates with Navy cheers as midshipmen prepare to battle Army in the annual fall football classic.

Above the altar of the Chapel is the Tiffany stained glass window named in honor of Admiral David Dixon Porter, known as the "Father of the modern Naval Academy."

midshipmen learn that when they have authority, they must fulfill the responsibilities that go along with it.

Over its one-hundred-and-fifty-year history, the Academy has produced many outstanding leaders. In the Spanish-American War, Admiral of the Navy George Dewey (Class of 1858) defeated the Spanish fleet at Manila Bay, and Rear Admiral William T. Sampson (Class of 1861) was the hero of Santiago. Lieutenant General John Archer Lejeune (Class of 1888) commanded the Second Marine Division in some of the most significant land battles in France in World War I, and, as the thirteenth commandant, led the Marine Corps for nine years, from 1920 to 1929. Fleet Admirals Leahy (Class of 1897), King (Class of 1901), Halsey (Class of 1904), and Nimitz (Class of 1905) were the architects of America's formidable naval victory in World War II. And Admiral Hyman Rickover (Class of 1922), known as the father of the nuclear navy, was a pioneer in naval nuclear technology.

In addition, graduates have distinguished themselves as scientists, diplomats, politicians, businessmen, and athletes. A. A. Michelson (Class of 1873) won the Nobel Prize for his measurement of the speed of light. William Sebald (Class of 1922) held the personal rank of ambassador and helped formulate the peace treaty with Japan after World War II. The Honorable James Earl Carter (Class of 1947) was the thirty-ninth president of the United States. Businessman H. Ross Perot (Class of 1953), founder of Electronic Data Systems, was a presidential candidate in 1992. Superstars Roger Staubach (Class of 1965) and David Robinson (Class of 1987) went on to extraordinarily successful professional athletic careers.

As the twenty-first century approaches, graduates can look back with pride over the first one hundred and fifty years. The contributions of alumni have enriched the Navy, the nation, and the world. From the earliest days of the Academy, when the country was just emerging as a force on the world scene, to America's superpower status of today, the Academy has always supplied the Navy with a corps of educated officers to defend its shores and protect its interests. With the fall of Communism and the end of the Cold War, new strategies will be developed to meet the country's changing needs. But the selfless dedication of young men and women who choose to meet the challenges of Academy life will continue to bring strength, skill, and renewal to the fleet and to the nation. They, in turn, will find fulfillment in the service they render. As President John F. Kennedy said, "I can imagine a no more rewarding career, and any man who may be asked in this century what he did to make his life worthwhile . . . can respond with a good deal of pride and satisfaction: 'I served in the United States Navy.'"

Plebes attempt to scale the twenty-one-foot Herndon Monument to begin the week-long celebration of Commissioning Week. The monument was erected to honor Commander William L. Herndon, who saved one hundred fifty passengers before he went down with his ship on September 12, 1857.

CHAPTER TWO

SETTING THE COURSE

The Early Years

It was an astonishing feat. Alexander Hamilton could not do it. John Quincy Adams could not do it. Even Thomas Jefferson met with failure. But there they were—officers, faculty, and fifty-six midshipmen assembled in a small recitation room on the grounds of old Fort Severn. At precisely 11:00 A.M. on October 10, 1845, Superintendent Franklin Buchanan declared the United States Naval School officially open. The man behind this miracle was George Bancroft.

Born in 1800 in Worcester, Massachusetts, Bancroft attended Phillips Academy at Exeter, New Hampshire, and enrolled at Harvard University at the age of thirteen. On graduation, he continued his studies in Germany and, before the age of twenty, received his doctorate from the University of Göttingen. While in Europe, he traveled extensively and met with the leading intellectuals of the day. Back in the United States, he and Joseph Green Cogswell founded the Round Hill School in Northampton, Massachusetts, an experimental boys' preparatory school based on the advanced educational philosophy of German schools. Selling his interest in the school in 1831, Bancroft began writing his ten-volume *History of the United States* and became active in the Democratic Party in Massachusetts. Because of his support for James Polk as Democratic candidate for the presidency in 1844, he was named Secretary of the Navy when Polk was elected.

Although Bancroft had no previous naval experience, he quickly understood that the new technology of steam-powered vessels would revolutionize the United States Navy. As an educator, he recognized that the old system of training officers was no longer sufficient and that the new officer would need a background in engineering and the principles of steam. For years, training had been based on the British system, in which boys, some as young as nine years old, were taken aboard ship and given practical experience. Conditions were harsh, discipline severe, and there was virtually no opportunity for even a rudimentary education. In an attempt to remedy the situation, Congress in 1813 ordered all ships of the line to appoint a schoolmaster for midshipmen, but the measure had very limited success. Schoolmasters were poorly paid, did not have the respect of the crew, and found that every other shipboard duty had precedence over time for studies. Some captains put limits on what could be taught, believing that it would undermine their authority if midshipmen learned ship's reckoning.

As early as 1783, John Paul Jones had proposed shore-based naval schools, and Alexander Hamilton, as Inspector General of the Army, had submitted to George Washington a plan for a military academy that would

A mid and his girl share a quiet moment at the Japanese Bell. Presented to Commodore Matthew C. Perry by the Regent of the Lew Chew Islands in 1854, the bell was given to the Academy by Perry's widow four years later. In 1986, it was returned to the people of Okinawa, and a replica now stands at the entrance to Bancroft Hall.

serve both the Army and the Navy. President John Adams forwarded the plan to Congress in 1800, but no action was taken. An academy for Army officers was established in 1802 at West Point, and six years later its superintendent, Colonel Jonathan Williams, attempted to include nautical astronomy, geography, and navigation to meet the needs of naval officers as well. Despite the fact that there were actually a few cadets warranted as midshipmen after 1812, the plan itself failed.

President John Quincy Adams was a strong advocate for a permanent school. In his first annual message to Congress in 1825, he stated, "The want of a naval school of instruction corresponding with the Military Academy at West Point, for the formation of scientific and accomplished officers, is felt with daily increasing aggravation." Although many supported the idea, its opponents killed the bills time after time, fearful of creating an elite corps of naval officers in a democratic society.

The need for a type of formal schooling was more than theoretical: beginning in 1819, midshipmen were required to pass an examination for promotion to lieutenant, the first such formal exam in the Navy. Midshipmen who were between cruises would attend cram schools while awaiting orders for their next ship. During the 1820s, two such schools grew up at East Coast Navy yards, one in New York and one in Norfolk, Virginia, and a third was established in 1833 in Boston. Midshipmen treated these waiting periods as if they were shore leave, preferring to spend their time exploring the attractions of the big cities. Discipline was lax, and they attended classes only when they chose to.

A fourth school at the Naval Asylum in Philadelphia was established in 1839 and was reorganized by William Chauvenet when the Navy assigned him to the school in 1842. The Philadelphia school enjoyed greater success because of the high quality of instructors and the strong leadership of Chauvenet. A mathematical genius educated at Yale, Chauvenet redesigned the curriculum and brought in chronometers, sextants, and charts for courses on seamanship and navigation. He envisioned a school where all midshipmen would spend two years in classroom studies acquiring the theoretical foundation they would need as officers. When George Bancroft became Secretary of the Navy in 1845, Professor Chauvenet forwarded his plan for a naval school to the new secretary.

Bancroft, a strong proponent of higher education for midshipmen, heartily endorsed Chauvenet's plan. Because of public indignation over conditions in the Navy and the outcry over the mutiny aboard the brig *Somers*, he felt the time was right for the establishment of a permanent school. In order to succeed where others had failed, he knew he had to enlist the support of influential naval officers and circumvent a Congressional veto. He appointed an advisory council composed of five men who were serving on the Board of Examiners at the Naval Asylum School—Commodore Matthew C. Perry, Commodore George C. Read, Commodore Thomas ap Catesby Jones, Captain E. A. F. Lavellette, and Captain Isaac Mayo. He shrewdly had them debate the courses of instruction and location of a naval school rather than whether or not it should be established in the first place.

With equal sagacity, Bancroft found a way to avoid asking Congress for approval. Learning of a little-used Army fort in Annapolis, Maryland, Bancroft asked Secretary of War William Marcy to transfer Fort Severn to the Navy. Since his son Samuel was an instructor at the Naval Asylum and a strong supporter of Chauvenet's plan, Secretary Marcy was happy to comply with the request. On August 15, 1845, Fort Severn officially became the property of the Navy, and Bancroft had the facilities for his school at no cost to his department.

His next challenge was to staff the school without going to Congress for an appropriation. At that time, the Navy employed twenty-two professors and three language teachers and received $28,272 per year to cover the cost of instructors. Bancroft ordered the worst instructors put on waiting orders, and their pay automatically stopped. Unable to support themselves and seeing no prospects for future employment, they left the Navy. Bancroft then sent his best teachers to Annapolis and used the money saved to operate the school.

Commander Franklin Buchanan was appointed the first superintendent. An inspired choice, he had become a midshipman at fifteen and had seen extensive service throughout the world. He was organized, determined, and respected by fellow officers. A stern disciplinarian, he was well-suited to deal with the group of diverse young men who reported on the first day of classes. He addressed the assembled midshipmen and stated that obedience, moral character, and temperance were to be the underlying principles of the Naval School. He expected of them "application, zeal, intelligence and correct deportment . . . [because] few if any now in the Service have had the advantages you are about to receive." At the close of the brief ceremony, Buchanan dismissed the midshipmen and classes began.

"Over the Wall—OTW." Midshipmen take "French Leave" to sample the delights of Annapolis after hours.

The First Fifteen Years

To teach the classes, Secretary Bancroft had put together a faculty of seven outstanding professors, four of whom had taught at the Naval Asylum School. William Chauvenet, whose plan for naval education had served as a model for the new school's curriculum, came to teach mathematics and navigation. His reputation and intellectual ability helped establish the scientific credentials of the fledgling institution. Lieutenant James Harmon Ward was appointed executive officer to Superintendent Buchanan, a post that since 1850 has been known as commandant. He also taught gunnery and steam engineering and wrote his *Manual of Naval Tactics*, which was used as a textbook by midshipmen for many years. Professor Henry Hayes Lockwood, who had assisted both Chauvenet and Ward at the Naval Asylum, was head of the Department of Natural Philosophy. A West Point graduate, Lockwood had been sent by Bancroft back to the Military Academy in July 1845 to report on its structure and organization. Much to the dismay of the midshipmen, he recommended infantry and artillery drills and even wrote a manual at arms for use at the Naval School. Passed Midshipman Samuel Marcy was Chauvenet's assistant in mathematics, and his support of the Naval School had helped persuade his father, the Secretary of War, to transfer Fort Severn to the Navy.

Three other distinguished men made up the original faculty. French-born Arsène Napoléon Girault, who taught French for over twenty years, was highly commended by Superintendent Buchanan in a letter to Secretary Bancroft: "his energy, zeal, and talent for teaching the French language, combined with his gentlemanly deportment, have gained for him the respect of all attached to the institution." George Jones, a schoolmaster aboard Navy ships and a commissioned chaplain, had been a strong proponent of a permanent naval school. He was appointed by Bancroft to head the Department of English Studies, which also included history and geography. In 1850, he became the Naval Academy's first chaplain. Surgeon John Lockwood, elder brother of Professor Henry Lockwood, taught chemistry and set up the School's first dispensary. Before he was detached in 1849, he had instituted courses in steam and international law.

As superintendent, Buchanan not only had to organize a curriculum and oversee the faculty, he also had to contend with the physical conditions of Fort Severn. Although the fort was only thirty-seven years old, the structures of the post were dilapidated and unsuited for use as a naval school. With virtually no funds available for renovation, Buchanan had to allocate buildings as best he could. The old brick bake house became midshipmen's quarters; the quartermaster's office became headquarters for the superintendent and the professors; and the unmarried enlisted men's barracks became recitation rooms and mess hall. The "wretched ramshackle" married men's quarters also housed midshipmen. Known as Apollo Row—home to the swells of the class—it was barely habitable, and its one fire in winter could not even melt the snow that blew in through cracks in the doors and windows. Rowdy Row quartered the more boisterous midshipmen, while the Abbey, abutting the School's north wall, was inhabited by the seemingly quiet and studious. In actuality, the "exemplary" young men of the Abbey were tunneling through the wall and carousing in town. There were not even enough buildings to accommodate all the faculty. Girault and Jones, the last to arrive, had to find lodgings in town.

The midshipmen who gathered that first day were a strange mix of seasoned sailors and inexperienced youth. The "Oldsters" had been to sea. Thirty-six had received their warrants as midshipmen in 1840 and would be eligible for promotion after a year's study at the School. Thirteen were of the Date of 1841 and would need additional time at sea before they could be promoted. The "Youngsters" had just been appointed acting midshipmen and entered the School directly from civilian life. So as not to be accused of running an academy for an aristocratic elite, Bancroft was forced to set low entrance requirements for acting midshipmen. They had only to be thirteen to sixteen years old, able to read and write, and have a basic understanding of geography and arithmetic—knowledge that could be gained at any village school.

The Oldsters were resentful of the strict standards that Buchanan set for study and deportment. They expected freedom to do as they pleased once they were released from shipboard discipline. Drinking was a major problem, as indicated by five courts-martial for intoxication between February and April 1846. Buchanan wrote to Secretary Bancroft, "As dissipation is the cause of all insubordination and misconduct in the Navy, and will if countenanced by me under any circumstance at this School, ruin its usefulness to the Service, and seriously injure its character with the country," he forbade it entirely.

Another problem he faced was that since Congress had not authorized the School to be a preliminary training academy, all those enrolled had to be active duty officers, and they could be called away to sea at any time. Others could be assigned throughout the academic year. Despite all the difficulties, the achievements of the Naval School were so impressive that Bancroft felt confident enough to tackle Congress in the summer of 1846. He requested $28,000 from the Navy Department "for repairs, improvements, and instruction at Ft. Severn, Annapolis, Maryland." The appropriation was passed, and the Naval School was officially recognized by law on August 13, 1846.

The academic foundation laid by Commander Buchanan stood the School in good stead through the tumultuous early years. He insisted in a letter to Professor Lockwood that the standards of education at the Naval School should be at least as rigorous as those at Princeton. Six days before the School opened, he established the Academic Board to set the policies regarding classes to be taught, hours of instruction, and examination procedures. Buchanan was firm in his belief that midshipmen should master the underlying principles of the subjects rather than commit specific texts to memory. Above all, he never lost sight of his primary goal—that of preparing officers for naval service. As at the old shore schools, a Board of Examiners arrived in June to test those midshipmen eligible for promotion. Courses were weighted according to their relative importance for duty at sea. Seamanship was rated five; mathematics and navigation, three; gunnery, two; French, two; natural philosophy, two; English, one; and chemistry, one. By the time Buchanan's request for active service during the Mexican War was approved in March 1847, the Naval School had been set on a steady course and was able to weather the instability of the war years.

With the declaration of war against Mexico, the midshipmen Date of 1840 were desperate to see action, and more than fifty petitioned to go to sea. By June, six had been ordered to duty, but the rest went to war only after they had taken their exams and received their commissions later in the summer. All told, ninety men from the Naval School served as officers in the Mexican War. The Navy performed well in the war, and both Congress and the American people once again acknowledged the importance of maintaining a strong, battle-ready force. The Naval School had proved its worth as well. Opponents were silenced as trained men from the School were quickly deployed and served capably as junior officers.

However, conditions at the school during the war were chaotic. Many midshipmen had their course of study shortened and were commissioned early. New arrivals regularly appeared and had to be assimilated into the already abbreviated program. Commander George P. Upshur, who took over as superintendent from Franklin Buchanan, was a capable officer but a poor disciplinarian. The midshipmen took advantage of his inability to enforce rules and regulations. After hours, many "Frenched out" (went over

The expanded Academy after Superintendent Cornelius K. Stribling's building program, as seen from the water in 1853.

the wall) and gathered in town taverns to drink far into the evening, toasting their secret societies. They often continued their parties when they returned to quarters; by morning, the rooms were littered with empty bottles, old cigars, and dirty dishes. One midshipman, Joseph Daniels (Date of 1841), smuggled in a monkey named Rory that he had brought back with him from the Congo. Rory became the mascot of the Owls, a drinking club, where he learned to chew tobacco and drink rum. Unfortunately, after one of the revels, Rory ate an entire box of matches and died. The Owls buried him with full military honors.

The authorities and the midshipmen waged a constant battle for control, the young men always looking for ways to gain the upper hand. At one point, Superintendent Upshur and Lieutenant Ward became baffled by the small quantity of milk that their cows were giving. Not until the end of the year did they learn that several midshipmen had been milking the cows nightly so that they could make punches in their rooms.

At times, individual professors were singled out for retribution or for practical jokes. Professor Henry Lockwood was a favorite target both because he was in charge of the detested military training and because he had a pronounced stutter. Midshipmen purposely misunderstood his commands. To avoid gunnery drill, they dismantled the big guns, scattered their parts throughout the grounds, and threw the linchpins into the bay. But on Saint Patrick's Day 1848, the midshipmen went too far. They hanged Lockwood in effigy, and Superintendent Upshur ordered the perpetrators of the deed court-martialed for insulting a superior officer. At the trial, the defense argued that the charge should be dismissed since professors were not officers, had never been warranted, and therefore were not the midshipmen's superiors. The court acknowledged the validity of the defense but ordered the midshipmen punished. To avoid future incidents, Congress passed a bill on August 3, 1848, which gave professors commissions and considerably increased their pay. Park Benjamin, Jr. (Class of 1867), said, "The youngsters sententiously remarked that for such an increase in pay, Lockwood could afford to be hanged in effigy every year."

Although the Upshur years were unsettled and disorderly, the strength of Buchanan's legacy and the leadership of Professors Chauvenet and Lockwood on the Academic Board sustained the School through its early days. By the end of Upshur's superintendency, Congress and the Navy had finally accepted the need for a shore-based school to train junior officers before they went to sea. Although it was recognized that the program had to include practical shipboard experience, more classroom time was needed as well. In

1850, the School was completely reorganized. Academic instruction was extended to two two-year periods, with three years of duty at sea in between. The curriculum was restructured, and the 4.0 grading system was introduced. Midshipmen were organized into gun crews and began to take leadership roles within the ranks. The entire disciplinary system was overhauled, and midshipmen who had two hundred or more demerits in any one year were dismissed. Clubs were banned; smoking, drinking, and dueling were forbidden; and any midshipman who married was automatically expelled. Commander Cornelius K. Stribling was appointed superintendent, and the School was renamed the United States Naval Academy.

In 1851, the sloop of war *Preble* was assigned to the Academy, making it unnecessary for midshipmen to interrupt their studies for extended periods at sea. Cruises on the *Preble* gave midshipmen practical training aboard ship just as summer encampments at West Point gave cadets military experience. Thus, on November 15, 1851, Secretary of the Navy William Graham approved a four-year continuous course of study at the end of which acting midshipmen would be granted a certificate of graduation and a midshipman's warrant. From this time forward, warrants were to be issued only to graduates of the Naval Academy. This was the beginning of the four-class system; as at West Point, those entering were called fourth classmen and those in their final year were first classmen. Acting midshipmen who entered in 1851 had the distinction of being "firsties" their entire four years.

Under Stribling, the ongoing building program continued, and new land was acquired. A chapel, observatory, and recitation hall were built, as well as additional quarters for the midshipmen. The quality of the construction was poor. Rear Admiral Edmund O. Matthews (Class of 1855) told of hearing a huge crash while studying one night when he was a midshipman. The wall in front of him suddenly collapsed, and he found himself sitting precariously on the second floor with one entire side of his room open to the cold night air. Eventually, all these buildings had to be replaced with more substantial structures.

Commander Louis Goldsborough took over as superintendent in November 1853, but even before he took command, he was a strong proponent of the Academy. When in April 1852 he was fitting out the frigate *Cumberland* for the Mediterranean, Goldsborough convinced the Secretary of the Navy not to order midshipmen from the Academy to the ship. He declared that he "would rather go to sea without a single midshipman than interrupt the studies of any at the Academy." As a result, the *Cumberland*'s officers had to perform duties usually relegated to midshipmen. Goldsborough's unselfish act set a significant precedent and upheld the importance of the Academy's training program.

One of America's naval heroes came to the Academy during Goldsborough's tenure. George Dewey was only one month shy of his sixteenth birthday when he entered on September 23, 1854, and he struggled through his first year, placing thirty-fifth out of the thirty-eight members of his class. His conduct grade was particularly low his first year, due in part to his immaturity. He was known to settle differences with his classmates by fighting and wrestling with them under the mess hall table. By his first class year, his studies and his deportment had improved so noticeably that he was named a first captain and graduated fifth in the class.

In later years, the promise of his Academy days was fulfilled. As a junior officer in the Civil War, he served under Admiral David Glasgow Farragut in the capture of New Orleans and under Rear Admiral David Dixon Porter in the fighting along the East Coast. During the Spanish-American War, he captured the entire Spanish fleet in Manila Bay without the loss of a single American seaman. In recognition of this victory and his distinguished naval career, Dewey was named Admiral of the Navy, a rank never held in the United States Navy before or since.

Rear Admiral Stephen B. Luce (Class of 1847, Date of 1841) as a mid in summer uniform with straw hat. Luce founded the Naval War College and wrote Seamanship, *the definitive work on the subject for nearly half a century.*

Another naval great was also a midshipman in the late 1850s. Alfred Thayer Mahan, son of the noted West Point professor Dennis Hart Mahan, entered the Academy as a youngster in 1857, the only midshipman ever allowed to skip his plebe year. Like Dewey, he was a "star man" in academics (he graduated second out of twenty) and a first captain his final year. However, he spent much of his first class year "in Coventry"—ostracized and given the silent treatment—because he broke the unspoken rule at the Academy and put classmates on report. Despite this trying experience, Mahan remained in the Navy for almost forty years and rose to the rank of rear admiral. He became a renowned historian, publishing *The Influence of Sea Power upon History* in 1890. He was a great naval strategist, and his book helped to stimulate the growth of navies from the turn of the century until World War I.

Seamanship by Stephen B. Luce (Class of 1847, Date of 1841) was also an influential work. Luce came to the Academy as assistant to the commandant in 1860 and was named head of the Department of Seamanship in 1862. Lacking an adequate text for the seamanship courses, he prepared a series of detailed lectures which he intended to publish. However, when he learned that Lieutenant Thomas T. Craven, a former commandant, was engaged in just such a project with Lieutenant Samuel Marcy, Luce put his plan aside.

As it happened, Craven's manuscript was lost when his ship, the *Housatanic*, was torpedoed during the Civil War. Luce's *Seamanship* became the standard work, bringing the subject into the age of steam.

The Civil War Years

The Civil War brought unrest and turmoil to the Naval Academy, as numerous midshipmen were torn by conflicting loyalties. Although Southerners felt strong ties to the Academy, their classmates, and the flag to which they had pledged their allegiance, many could not deny their devotion to their home states. Coming together in darkened rooms evening after evening, they debated by lantern light their course of action should their states secede. Over suppers smuggled in from Dauté's tavern, upperclassmen searched for news from local papers and shared with their brethren impassioned letters from home. Eighteen members of the Class of 1861 decided to petition Secretary of the Navy Isaac Toucey. These first classmen, only months away from graduation, asked the secretary to grant "our Certificates, or equivalents, as may be deemed most proper, when it shall be incumbent upon us to resign and return to our homes." Toucey ignored their plea.

Plebes, housed on the school ship *Constitution*, carried on their own debates. Unlike the upperclassmen who had been insulated at the Academy for several years, these newly arrived young men had been embroiled in the issues and the discord sweeping the nation, and sectional sentiment ran high. Nevertheless, bonds among classmates remained strong. Acting Midshipman William E. Yancey of Alabama was torn between his desire to stay at the Academy and his loyalty to his state when Alabama seceded from the Union on January 11, 1861. He received an ultimatum from his father, W. L. Yancey, the leader of the states' rights movement in Alabama: "Resign or I will disown you." Midshipman Yancey joined the Confederate States Navy and lost his life at the Battle of Ball's Bluff.

One midshipman's mother actually resigned for him. Robley D. "Fighting Bob" Evans (Class of 1864), though born in Virginia, decided to "stick by 'The Old Flag' and let my family ties look after themselves, and so informed my mother, who was much grieved and shamed by my determination. She finally wrote my resignation, sent it to the Navy Department, where it was accepted, and without previous warning, I found myself out of the service." Fortunately for the Union, the Navy reinstated him. Evans saw action in the Civil War, served as captain of the *Iowa* in the Spanish-American War, and later commanded Teddy Roosevelt's Great White Fleet.

Each Southerner who left did so only after an agonizing struggle with his conscience, and classmates sadly and reluctantly accepted the decision. When honor man Sardine Stone resigned in January 1861, he was surrounded by his fellows and escorted to the gate. At his side was his good friend William T. Sampson, who went on to become superintendent of the Academy and hero of the Spanish-American War. As they walked by the officers' quarters, Commandant C. R. P. Rodgers rushed out to investigate what he thought was a riot. Sampson told him, "We are merely bidding our classmate good-by," and Rodgers sorrowfully told them to proceed.

With the surrender of Fort Sumpter on April 14, 1861, Commandant Rodgers read the "Articles of War" to the assembled midshipmen. The Academy prepared to defend itself from possible invasion by Southern sympathizers. Word had reached Captain George Blake, the superintendent, that armed bands from Baltimore intended to commandeer the *Constitution*, "Old Ironsides" herself. They boasted that they would make her the flagship of the Confederate Navy and use the Academy as a base for attacks against Washington. All classes were suspended, and Superintendent Blake ordered howitzers placed at the gates, Academy guns spiked, and arms and ammunition taken aboard the *Constitution*. In a letter to the Secretary of the Navy, Blake stated that the Academy "is not defensible against a superior force, and that the only force at my command consists of the students at the Academy, many of whom are little boys, and some of whom are citizens of the seceded States." Blake's orders were to save the *Constitution* at all costs, and if the Academy were taken, to evacuate the midshipmen aboard the ship and sail to New York or Philadelphia. If all else failed, he was to blow up the *Constitution* and all the munitions stored on her rather than let her fall into enemy hands.

When Maryland secessionists destroyed railroad bridges outside Baltimore and the Norfolk Navy Yard was set afire, Blake prepared for what he thought would be a certain attack on Annapolis. Midshipmen were armed and patrolled the grounds. Even those who had tendered their resignations faithfully performed their duties while awaiting official notice of release. They manned sentry posts on the waterfront, and some accompanied the commandant on his nightly rounds. The schooner *Rainbow*, in the charge of Lieutenant Edmund O. Matthews, was sent out to warn of the approach of any suspicious vessels. At one o'clock in the morning of April 21, the ferryboat *Maryland* appeared offshore. Matthews, fearing that the attack was at hand, put the Academy on alert and boarded the steamer. To his relief, he discovered that the *Maryland* was transporting the Eighth Massachusetts

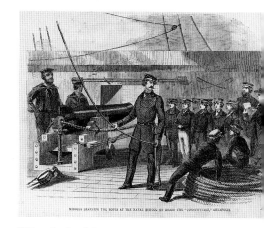

When the Confederates boasted that they would make the venerable "Old Ironsides" the flagship of their Navy, Superintendent Blake was ordered to defend her at all costs.

Regiment under the command of General Benjamin Butler. When Superintendent Blake welcomed the general, an amusing interchange ensued. As Butler later recounted, Blake tearfully exclaimed:

> "Thank God, thank God! Won't you save the *Constitution?*"
>
> I did not know that he referred to the ship *Constitution*, and I answered, "Yes, that is what I am here for."
>
> "Are those your orders? Then the old ship is safe."
>
> "I have no orders," said I. "I am carrying on this war now on my own hook. I cut loose from my orders when I left Philadelphia. What do you want me to do to save the *Constitution?*"
>
> "I want some sailormen," he answered, "for I have no sailors; I want to get her out and get her afloat."
>
> "Oh, well," said I, "I have plenty of sailormen from the town of Marblehead, where their fathers built the *Constitution*."

The Eighth Massachusetts joined by the Seventh Regiment of New York City landed and took over the Academy buildings. It became clear to Blake that he had to evacuate the midshipmen. The Class of 1861 gathered together for the last time and passed a pipe of peace among them. They vowed eternal friendship even though they might face each other across enemy lines. The duty officer reported them for smoking in quarters, but, under the circumstances, Commandant Rodgers dismissed the charge. Before boarding the *Constitution*, the battalion formed up in front of the Recitation Hall. The band played "The Star-Spangled Banner" and "Hail Columbia" as all stood at attention. Commandant Rodgers made a last, impassioned appeal to the Southerners. "Be true to the Flag, young Gentlemen! Be true to the Flag." He then dismissed those who could not in good conscience head north. Classmates embraced and wept on each other's shoulders. Then the order came to embark, and the *Constitution* set out for New York harbor to await word of the school's new location.

Blake immediately sent representatives to Secretary of the Navy Gideon Welles and Secretary of War Edwin Stanton requesting the transfer of Fort Adams in Newport, Rhode Island, to the Navy. Since the fort was unoccupied and on the water, Blake thought it a suitable temporary home for the Academy. His emissaries called on both men at home very early in the morning in order to impress upon them the urgency of the situation. Both men agreed, and the transfer took place on April 27, 1861. The *Constitution* arrived in Newport on May 9 along with the *Baltic*, carrying the officers, faculty, and their families. The next day, the first, second, and third classmen were ordered to sea, and only the fourth class remained in Newport when classes resumed on May 13. Because of the large number of resignations by Southerners and the wartime expansion of the Navy, the need for officers was acute. By the end of the month, it seemed likely that even the fourth class would be sent to war, and had not Commandant Rodgers resisted, the school would have ceased to exist.

When the new fourth class arrived in September, they were housed on the *Constitution*, and the third class moved first to Fort Adams, which proved inadequate, and then to the Atlantic House. Within five days, Academy officials attempted to transform this once gracious summer hotel facing Newport's Public Square into suitably spartan quarters for the acting midshipmen. Ornate mirrors, carpets, overstuffed chairs—all vestiges of elegance and comfort—were removed. Ship models and naval trophies carefully transported from Annapolis were displayed in the main hall, along with the Academy's treasured "Don't Give Up the Ship" battle flag flown by Oliver Hazard Perry during the War of 1812. As utilitarian and military as its interior became, Atlantic House could never be the perfect environment for midshipmen. Without enclosing walls and gates, it was easy for midshipmen to ignore the designated "Yard" limits and go freely into town. They climbed down the old hotel's drainpipes and patronized local restaurants and taverns. One offered oyster pies reminiscent of those of Dauté's, in Annapolis, and others tempted midshipmen with cream pies laced with sherry. Finally, in an attempt to placate Academy authorities, the town passed an ordinance threatening tavern keepers with fines and imprisonment for serving midshipmen without permission.

On the whole, Newport was delighted to have the Naval Academy in its midst. The presence of the dashing young men renewed the social life of this once popular resort. Local families opened their homes and held dances for them. On Saturday afternoons, young ladies could often be seen aboard the yacht *America* with their midshipmen escorts. In addition, the presence of the Academy afforded the town a sense of security. Superintendent Blake installed guns at Fort Adams, and infantry and artillery drills were held near Ochre Point. During the summers, the acting midshipmen patrolled the coastline to guard it from Confederate raiders. With the possibility that they might be captured, their status needed to be clarified. By agreement, a midshipman was worth seven ordinary seamen or seven Army or Marine Corps privates. However, there was no set exchange value for an acting midship-

A navigation class takes place at the old stone mill outside the gate of the Naval Academy at Newport in 1863.

man. Therefore, in July 1862, Congress eliminated the grade of acting midshipman and granted each student the rank of midshipman on entering the Academy.

The curriculum during the Newport years emphasized gunnery and navigation and other practical subjects to prepare midshipmen for entry into wartime service. With most of the library's books still packed in crates and much of the laboratory equipment in storage, classroom standards could not approach those at Annapolis. Superintendent Blake supplied the only real continuity. His request for sea duty was denied because Secretary of the Navy Gideon Welles felt his leadership was crucial for the Academy. Commandants changed frequently, and so many officers were sent off to war that the faculty became predominantly civilian. Discipline was hard to maintain. Midshipmen fenced in the hallways, hid bottles of whiskey under floorboards, played cards, and secreted tobacco in hollowed-out books.

In October 1862, the sailing frigate *Santee* joined the *Constitution* in providing living quarters for midshipmen. Conditions on the dark and overcrowded school ships were poor, allowing little privacy and no place to study. The *Santee* was especially dismal; once back in Annapolis, it served as a prison ship for midshipmen who had committed major conduct offenses.

In spite of all the difficulties—the removal of the Academy to Newport, the disruption of studies, and early graduation—Academy men served valiantly in the war. As Commander Samuel Dupont said of three members of the Class of 1862, they "sustained the reputation and exhibited the benefits of the Naval Academy, the training of which only could make such valuable officers of such young men." One of the most daring young officers was William B. Cushing, a member of the Class of 1861, who resigned from the Academy in his first class year. He led a number of bold raids, always displaying, as one of his citations read, "coolness, courage and gallantry." His most famous deed took place on October 27, 1864. Heading up the Roanoke River in a small steam launch, Cushing blew up the Confederate ram *Albemarle*, commanded by Academy graduate Alexander F. Worley (Class of 1846, Date of 1840). This ironclad had challenged Union dominance in the North Carolina sounds and had engaged a number of federal ships. Cushing's launch was fired on, and he himself, wounded in the wrist, had to swim to shore, barely making it back alive.

Two members of the Academy's first graduating class had unusual careers during the Civil War. Both William Nelson and Samuel P. Carter (Class of 1846, Date of 1840) felt that they could serve more effectively in the Army. They were granted Army commissions, and each rose to the rank

"Damn the torpedoes! Full steam ahead." Admiral Farragut takes Mobile Bay for the Union, September, 1864.

of major general. Nelson lost his life in a dispute with a fellow officer in 1862. Carter survived the war and subsequently returned to the Navy, served as commandant of the Academy from 1870 to 1873, and retired as a rear admiral—the only man ever to have been both an admiral and a general.

The Academy's own West Point graduate, Professor Henry Lockwood, who had been a member of the faculty at Annapolis from the very beginning, was granted special permission by the Navy Department to rejoin the Army. As a brigadier general, he led a number of expeditions and commanded a brigade in the Battle of Gettysburg. At the conclusion of the war, he returned to teach once again at the Naval Academy.

Two of Lockwood's colleagues on the Academy's first faculty lost their lives early in the war. Commander James H. Ward, who had been executive officer to Superintendent Buchanan, was charged with maintaining a line of communication by water to Washington. On June 27, 1861, he was shot by a Confederate sharpshooter and became the first Union naval officer to be killed in the war. Lieutenant Commander Samuel Marcy lost his life in an unfortunate accident while in command of the USS *Vincennes* in January 1862. He died from the recoil of a defective howitzer while bombarding an enemy vessel attempting to run the Union blockade at the southeast pass of the Mississippi.

The Academy's first superintendent, Franklin Buchanan, chose to cast his lot with the South. He was appointed captain in the Confederate States Navy, and in February 1862 he was given command of the ironclad CSS *Virginia*, constructed from the hull of the scuttled USS *Merrimac*. The next month he took the Chesapeake Bay Squadron to Hampton Roads, Virginia, where the Union had established a blockade at the mouth of the James River. On March 8, Buchanan launched a surprise attack on the Union squadron. In the engagement, Buchanan sank the USS *Cumberland* and damaged several other vessels, including the *Congress*, commanded by Lieutenant Joseph B. Smith (Class of 1847, Date of 1841), who had been a midshipman at the Academy under Buchanan. And, as so often happened in the Civil War, brother fought against brother. McKean Buchanan, the purser on board the *Congress*, was fighting on the deck when it was run aground by his brother. During the encounter, Franklin Buchanan was wounded in the thigh. As a result, he was unable to command the *Virginia* the next day in the historic battle against the *Monitor*, commanded by future Academy Superintendent John L. Worden. Buchanan, promoted to admiral, became the highest ranking member of the Confederate States Navy and later in the war was placed in charge of the defense of Mobile Bay.

Palm trees and garlands transformed the gymnasium in old Fort Severn into an elegant ballroom during June Week, 1869, at "Porter's Dancing Academy."

Two other brothers, both with ties to the Academy, also chose different sides during the war. Commander Foxhall A. Parker, who later became the Academy's ninth superintendent, remained with the Union. His younger brother Lieutenant William H. Parker left his post in the Department of Seamanship when Virginia seceded and joined the Confederate States Navy. As did Buchanan, he took part in the Battle of Hampton Roads, but he is best known as the superintendent of the Confederate States Naval Academy, the position he assumed in the fall of 1863. The school was located on the CSS *Patrick Henry*, moored near Drewry's Bluff on the James River, a few miles southeast of Richmond. Patterned after the United States Naval Academy at Annapolis, the CSNA had a comprehensive program that included English, mathematics, and modern languages as well as courses in seamanship, gunnery, and navigation. Midshipmen received their practical training by joining naval expeditions and firing ships' guns against the enemy. Despite the turmoil of the times, the CSNA gave the appearance of an institution with a long tradition that would continue far into the future. Under Parker's leadership, this academy sent out ordnance and drill officers to the Confederate Navy until Richmond fell in April 1865.

Lieutenant John T. Wood (Class of 1853, Date of 1847) taught before the war at the U.S. Naval Academy along with William Parker. He, too, left in April 1861 and joined the Confederate Navy. As commander of the *Tallahassee*, he led a nineteen-day raid and destroyed twenty-six enemy vessels in the summer of 1864. James Iredell Waddell (Class of 1847, Date of 1841), fiercely devoted to the Confederacy, captained the commerce raider *Shenandoah*. In the course of the war, he captured thirty-eight Union ships, and in June 1865, even though Lee had already surrendered at Appomattox, Waddell continued to fight, destroying the entire unarmed New England whaling fleet in the Bering Sea.

All told, more than forty acting midshipmen resigned from the Academy to go South. Ninety-five graduates left the United States Navy to serve the Confederacy, while four hundred remained loyal to the Union. Because the Academy had only been in existence for fifteen years when the war began, its graduates were young men who served as junior officers, most as lieutenants. Some became lieutenant commanders and, by war's end, a few attained the rank of commander. The greatly expanded Navy needed so many new officers that over eight hundred and fifty young men were admitted to the Academy during the four wartime years. This "hump" of young officers, all the same age and all the same rank, created a bottleneck and held up career advancement and promotion until the turn of the century.

The huge influx of midshipmen and the unsuitable setting in the heart of Newport caused Secretary of the Navy Gideon Welles to call for the Academy's return to Annapolis as early as 1862. Because the Army needed the site, the request was refused. The business community of Newport campaigned energetically to retain the Academy, although many citizens (especially fathers of young ladies) were unhappy with what they called the "return of the middy-evil age." Several other cities petitioned to become the Academy's permanent home—Perth Amboy, New Jersey; New London, Connecticut; Portsmouth, New Hampshire; and Portland, Maine. But in an amendment to the naval appropriations bill signed into law on May 21, 1864, Congress decreed that the Academy would return to Annapolis by the start of the 1865 academic year. When the last midshipman sailed away on his practice cruise in June 1865, the Academy's Newport days officially came to an end.

The Superintendency of David Dixon Porter

To any who had known it in its prewar days, the Academy in the fall of 1865 was a sorry sight. Because of its access to the water routes and rail lines that connected Washington with the major cities on the East Coast, Annapolis held strategic importance for the Army. Early in the war, it served as a staging area for expeditions to the South, and later the Naval Academy and Saint John's College became hospitals for the sick and wounded sent from the front. The grounds were almost destroyed. "The long row of willow trees that fringed the bay front had been eaten by the cavalry horses, wagon ruts ruined the lawns, sheds had been built on the parade grounds, to serve as beer rooms and sutler's shops. Even the . . . Superintendent's house had been turned into a billiard saloon." To the new superintendent, Rear Admiral David Dixon Porter, fell the task of rebuilding the Academy and reestablishing its reputation.

Son of the famous Commodore David Porter and foster brother of David Glasgow Farragut, David Dixon Porter served his first shipboard duty at age eleven, entered the Mexican Navy along with his father, and at fourteen was taken prisoner in Cuba. On his release, he rejoined the United States Navy. During the Civil War, his feats earned him four votes of thanks from Congress, and he rose to the rank of rear admiral. As Academy superintendent, Admiral Porter brought about sweeping changes. He purchased several tracts of land to expand Academy grounds and built additional classrooms, a brick chapel, and the five-story "New Quarters" to house the midshipmen. It was under Porter that the beloved figurehead from the USS *Delaware*, known to generations of midshipmen as Tecumseh, was given to the Academy.

Having just fought the Civil War, Porter emphasized the practical aspects of the curriculum and brought in brilliant young veterans as faculty, including Lieutenant Commander Stephen B. Luce as commandant. He reorganized the battalion, designed new uniforms, and instituted dress parades in the evenings, both spring and fall. The honor concept was introduced and the disciplinary system revised, allowing midshipmen to walk off demerits for many offenses. Porter briefly tried "night patrols," having offenders patrol the grounds in the middle of the night. This punishment proved to be particularly unpopular with professors, who not only had to put up with exhausted midshipmen in class but sometimes found themselves arrested as "trespassers" as they returned home late at night.

Under Porter, the Naval Academy took on many characteristics of American collegiate life. Individual classes began to establish their own identities. They adopted class colors and class rings and, later, class songs. Athletic activities, which had always been limited, were now actively encouraged. Classes formed their own baseball teams—Nautical (Class of 1867), Severn (Class of 1868), Monitor (Class of 1869), Santee (Class of 1870)—and challenged each other to Saturday afternoon games. The nine-foot-thick walls of old Fort Severn were blasted away, and the shell that remained was converted into a gymnasium for the midshipmen. Superintendent Porter enthusiastically participated in athletic activities himself, using the gymnasium equipment. Once he even boxed with a midshipman, an unheard of act for one of such exalted rank. On the practice cruise of 1868, midshipmen sailed to West Point and challenged the cadets to baseball and rowing. An Army officer who observed the competition later wrote, "At this time there was no organized sport at West Point. . . . Somewhat stirred by a visit of the training ship of the Naval Academy, there developed an appreciation of the value of sport as a tonic morally and physically."

Social life flourished at the Academy. Weekly hops were held in the Lyceum with young ladies of Annapolis and officers and their wives in attendance. Special occasions were celebrated with formal balls. So popular were these events that some referred drolly to the school as "Porter's Dancing Academy." Superintendent Porter's influence was assuredly great, and his innovations so extensive that he has been called by many the father of the modern Naval Academy.

After Porter's departure in December 1869, the decline of the Navy began to have an impact on the Academy. From more than seven hundred ships at the end of the Civil War, the fleet had been reduced to thirty-one. Obviously, few officer billets were available, and positions and promotions were scarce for the many young veterans already in the ranks, not to mention the graduating midshipmen. To make matters worse, in 1870 Congress passed legislation denying midshipmen their official rank and reclassifying them as cadet-midshipmen or cadet-engineers. Morale at the Academy sank. Under the administration of Superintendents John L. Worden and C. R. P. Rodgers, the lighthearted pranks and tricks of previous years began to degenerate into cruel and vicious hazing. Even the passage of a law against hazing in 1874 could not stop the practice, and it continued to plague the Academy.

It was also in this decade that the first African-Americans were admitted, but none completed the course. Not until Wesley A. Brown was commissioned in 1949 did the Academy have its first black graduate.

In 1873, fifteen officers and faculty members independently founded the United States Naval Institute. Frustrated by the country's unwillingness to apply and explore the lessons in naval technology and warfare learned in the Civil War, they met monthly to pursue scientific advances. The following year, their papers and articles were collected and disseminated throughout the naval community. The Naval Institute's *Proceedings*, still published today, is a highly respected professional journal.

One of the Institute's founders, Commodore Foxhall A. Parker, a scholar of naval history and an author of several books on naval tactics, took over as superintendent in July 1878. During his administration, Albert A. Michelson (Class of 1873) performed his famous experiment to measure the speed of light while instructing a physics class at the Academy. In 1907, Michelson won the Nobel Prize for this work, the first American to be so honored.

After less than a year in office, Parker died during June Week, 1879, and was succeeded by Rear Admiral George B. Balch. Rear Admiral C. R. P. Rodgers once again assumed the helm of the Academy two years later, the only man to serve as superintendent twice. Captain Francis M. Ramsay took over in 1881, determined to reverse the decline of the preceding decade. He instituted curriculum reforms, established a conduct grade, and demanded

President Ulysses S. Grant, a personal friend of Superintendent David Dixon Porter and a frequent visitor to the Naval Academy, handed out diplomas at the 1869 graduation exercises.

strict adherence to rules and regulations. In an attempt to discourage hazing, he quartered midshipmen by divisions rather than by classes. Accustomed to the more relaxed standards of the preceding administrations, midshipmen resented Ramsay's reforms. Making matters worse, Congress passed the Naval Appropriations Act of August 1882, severely limiting the number of graduates who would receive commissions. Intended to reduce the oversupply of junior officers, the "hump" left over from the Civil War, the Act required midshipmen to return to Annapolis after spending two years at sea to take final examinations. The few billets available were then awarded to those who stood high in the order of merit. Others, though highly qualified, were given honorable discharges from the service. However, the Act did specify that graduates could accept Marine Corps commissions, provided that openings existed. With this sanction, Congress for the first time recognized the Academy's role in preparing officers for the Corps.

All these changes caused morale to plummet at the Academy. Several incidents occurred during the academic year of 1882–83 that Superintendent Ramsay felt challenged his authority. At one time, he confined the entire first class to the prison ship *Santee* and stripped several midshipmen officers of their rank. All but two others resigned their leadership positions in protest. Eventually the midshipmen apologized and were allowed to return to their quarters, but trouble resurfaced at graduation. Ramsay heard a rumor that the battalion planned to remain silent when the midshipmen who had not resigned their positions received their diplomas. He therefore forbade any cheering at all during the ceremony. When the honor man's name was read, many gave him the traditional cheer, and Ramsay exploded. He ordered those who had disobeyed to step forward and had them marched off to the *Santee* in front of their bewildered families and friends. Although those under arrest were released within an hour, the graduation was spoiled, and the class cancelled its traditional ball.

Beginning with Ramsay, who graduated in the Class of 1856, all superintendents have been Academy alumni. Commander William T. Sampson, who stood first in the Class of 1861, took over in September 1886. By this time, the Navy had once again begun to command the respect of the nation, which was reflected in improved morale at the Academy. Sampson was a forward-looking officer who emphasized the practical application of new technology in preparing midshipmen for the modern Navy. He also instituted the aptitude for service grade, a predictor of a student's future performance in the fleet. Altogether, Sampson served four "tours" at the Academy—as a midshipman, assistant professor, department head, and su-

Midshipmen studying in their room, 1869.

perintendent—but he is best known for his role in the Spanish-American War a decade later.

The 1890s brought stability to the Academy. During those years, a number of treasured traditions originated. In the fall of 1890, midshipmen (called at this time naval cadets) challenged West Point to a football game. They traveled up the Hudson and soundly defeated the cadets on their own ground, 24-0. In 1892, blue and gold were adopted as official Academy colors—blue for the waters of the sea and gold for the braid worn proudly by naval officers. The *Lucky Bag*, the Academy's yearbook, was first published in 1894, and in 1899, the Academy crest, designed by Park Benjamin, Jr., was adopted.

The peace of these years was shattered with the destruction of the battleship *Maine* in Havana harbor on February 15, 1898. Captain William T. Sampson headed a court of inquiry to determine the cause of the explosion. The board ruled that the ship had been destroyed by a mine, and on April 25, with shouts of "Remember the *Maine!*" ringing through the country, America declared war on Spain.

Unlike earlier wars fought by the United States, the Spanish-American War was essentially fought at sea, and everyone at the Academy was eager to see action. The Class of 1898 received their diplomas at noon formation on April 2 and immediately left for the fleet. A month later, the second class joined them. Those who stayed behind were eager for active duty as well, and that summer, forty-six members of the Class of 1900 and twenty-nine of the Class of 1901 went to war, too. The war had two objectives: to immobilize the Spanish fleet in the Philippines and to drive Spain from the Western Hemisphere. It showcased the brilliance of Academy graduates who had become the senior officers of the Navy. Commodore George Dewey (Class of 1858) steamed into Manila Bay in command of the Asiatic Squadron. In the early hours of May 1, he ordered the captain of the cruiser *Olympia* to begin the battle with his now-famous words, "You may fire when you are ready, Gridley." When the smoke cleared six hours later, Admiral Montojo surrendered, and Dewey took the Philippines without the loss of a single American life.

In Cuba, Spanish Admiral Cervera had taken refuge in the harbor of Santiago. The North Atlantic Squadron, under the command of Rear Admiral William T. Sampson, blockaded the harbor. When Cervera tried to escape, a battle ensued, and the entire Spanish fleet was destroyed on July 3. Sampson wired Washington, "The fleet under my command offers the nation as a Fourth of July present, the whole of Cervera's fleet." Spanish

The three most famous admirals of the nineteenth century—Admiral David Glasgow Farragut, Admiral David Dixon Porter, and Admiral George Dewey (Class of 1858).

With the smoke of burning Spanish ships behind them, sailors of Rear Admiral William T. Sampson's (Class of 1861) fleet give thanks for their resounding victory over Admiral Cervera.

casualties numbered over 450, and the 638 enlisted men remaining were taken prisoner. Along with fifty of their officers, many of whom had been saved from their burning ships, they were transferred to the *St. Louis*. They sailed to Portsmouth, New Hampshire, where it was decided to send the officers to Annapolis and hold them at the Naval Academy.

On the afternoon of July 16, the *St. Louis* dropped anchor near the Academy wharf, and the Spanish prisoners were ferried to shore. An official greeting party, including a Marine guard, met them, and Admiral Cervera was received with the honors due his rank. By terms of their parole, the Spaniards could freely roam the Academy grounds and the city of Annapolis from 8:00 A.M. until sundown. Superintendent Frederick McNair (Class of 1857) treated his charges more as honored guests than as prisoners and went to great lengths to protect them from reporters and photographers.

The town opened its arms to the Spaniards as well. They attended mass regularly at Saint Mary's Church in Duke of Gloucester Street, and Cervera and Father Kautz, the rector of the church, developed a high regard for one another. The prisoners were especially welcomed by the merchants in town, who were amused at the run on curling irons, which the Spaniards used to groom their mustaches. With the eligible men off to war, young ladies were delighted to entertain the Spanish officers, and a round of parties filled the summer. One particularly aristocratic young man wrote home about a beautiful Annapolis belle. His horrified mother wired Admiral Cervera, demanding that her Luis be sent home immediately, completely disregarding the fact that he was a prisoner of war. Fortunately for her, the Secretary of the Navy released the prisoners on August 31, 1898, and a week later Luis, still unbetrothed, and the others headed home to Spain. As a Naval Academy instructor later wrote, "It had been a strange war, and a still stranger captivity. What had begun with bursting shells and blazing ships ended in ice cream, cake and moonlight walks."

For its astounding victories in the Spanish-American War, the Navy was honored throughout the nation, and the Academy was celebrated for the leaders it had sent forth to command the fleet. In a little more than fifty years, the Academy had grown from an unlikely assemblage of dilapidated buildings and rough seamen to a treasured institution hailed as the symbol of the Navy's preeminence in the new century. From his "bully pulpit," President Theodore Roosevelt exuberantly proclaimed the country's emergence on the world scene and looked to the Navy and the Academy to guard its interests and to protect its shores.

Atlantic House in Newport, Rhode Island, was an old summer hotel that became the temporary home of the Naval Academy during the Civil War.

Gathered on the steps of New Quarters, midshipmen wear naval and athletic uniforms of the 1890s.

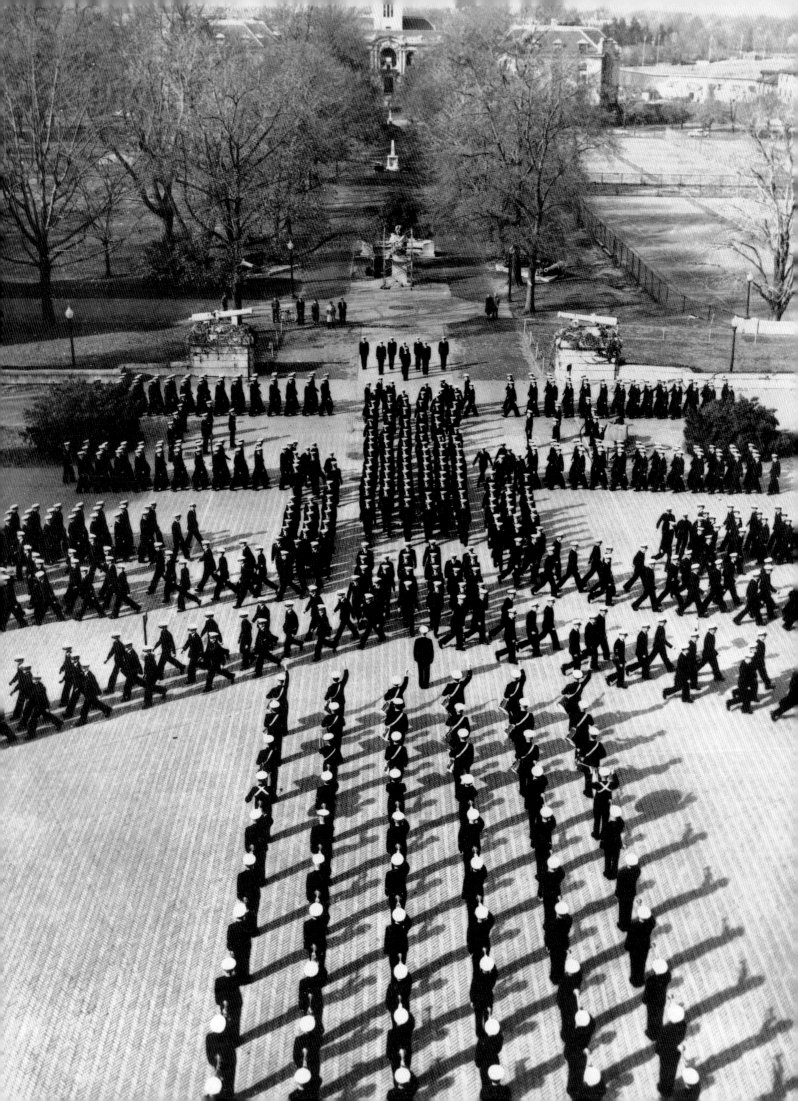

CHAPTER THREE

FULL SPEED AHEAD:

Into the Twentieth Century

The Spanish-American War marked the nation's entry into the Age of Imperialism. With vast new territories to administer and protect, the country needed a greatly expanded Navy to patrol the waters and secure its possessions. Between the Spanish-American War and World War I, Congress appropriated large sums of money for new battleships, cruisers, and other vessels, setting off a boom in shipbuilding. On December 16, 1907, the Great White Fleet under the command of Rear Admiral Robley D. "Fighting Bob" Evans (Class of 1864) set sail on an around-the-world voyage to demonstrate America's new-found naval strength and its intention to maintain a presence in the Pacific. Permanent bases were established in Hawaii, the Philippines, and Guam. With Theodore Roosevelt as president, the nation enthusiastically embraced its emergence as a major player in world affairs and glorified the Navy for its victories at Santiago and Manila Bay.

The growth of the Navy necessitated growth at the Academy as well. To meet the ever increasing demand for junior officers, the brigade was expanded from four companies to eight in 1903, and beginning that year, five classes were graduated early to fill the billets in the fleet. Not only were Academy facilities inadequate to house and train the larger brigade, the buildings were antiquated and the sanitary system nearly ineffective. Colonel Robert Means Thompson (Class of 1868), a member of the Board of Visitors, commissioned New York architect Ernest Flagg to draw up plans to renovate the Academy. Flagg quickly realized that renovation was hopeless—it was necessary to redesign and rebuild the entire school. His plans called for a number of buildings in the Beaux-Arts style with Greco-Roman detailing, all connected by tree-lined walks. A one-million-dollar appropriation by Congress in 1898 allowed work to begin on the new Academy the next year. Within the next decade, the modern Academy took shape. Bancroft, Dahlgren, Macdonough, Isherwood, Mahan, Maury, and Sampson Halls, along with the Chapel, the Officers' Club, and the superintendent's house, were completed, and a number of added acres enlarged the grounds.

For those in authority, the prolonged period of construction made it more difficult to keep things running smoothly. Midshipmen, as is their wont, found numerous ways to take advantage of the disruptions. One famous story concerned future Fleet Admiral Chester W. Nimitz, who was a midshipman at this time and graduated in the Class of 1905. He and his classmates were the first to move into the one completed wing of Bancroft Hall in the fall of 1904. They soon discovered they could go out onto the roof, where they could hold beer parties. Even when they threw the empty

Midshipmen form up in T-Court in direct line with Tecumseh, the Mexican and Macedonian Monuments, and the Clock Tower of Mahan Hall.

Seamanship training aboard a full-rigged school ship.

bottles down onto the building materials below, they went undetected by the Jimmy-Legs, the guards.

One Saturday afternoon, Nimitz drew the short straw and had to go to town to pick up the beer. He took an empty suitcase to the usual place of supply, the back room of a tailor shop on Maryland Avenue. Disregarding a customer who was having a suit fitted, he filled the case and returned to the Academy. Once through the main gate, he breathed a sigh of relief; that night, he greatly enjoyed the party. Monday morning, however, he was shocked to discover that the other customer at the tailor shop was his new navigation professor, Lieutenant Commander Levi Calvin Bertolette (Class of 1887). For days, Nimitz was convinced that he was about to be dismissed from the Academy, but Commander Bertolette never mentioned the incident. As Admiral Nimitz later said, "This escapade taught me a lesson on how to behave for the remainder of my stay at the Academy. It also taught me to look with lenient and tolerant eye on first offenders."

Years later, a first class midshipman wrote to Nimitz asking for stories of the admiral's Academy days. Nimitz wanted to share this episode but wondered if it was an appropriate example for midshipmen. He wrote to Commandant Charles S. Minter, Jr. (Class of 1937), and asked his advice. The commandant told him by all means to tell the story. He felt it was important to show midshipmen the human side of a great leader.

The first decade of the twentieth century also brought a renewed interest in the Navy's early history. The United States' ambassador to France, General Horace Porter, spent six years attempting to locate the burial place of John Paul Jones, America's first naval hero, who had died in France on July 18, 1792. General Porter, a West Point graduate and amateur historian, discovered Jones's grave in what had been the northeast corner of the old Cemetery Saint-Louis in Paris. Experts identified the body, which had been preserved in alcohol and sealed in a lead coffin. With full military honors accorded by the French government, Jones's coffin was brought to the warship *Brooklyn* at Cherbourg, France. A squadron of American and French ships escorted the *Brooklyn* across the Atlantic to Annapolis.

In a solemn ceremony in July 1905, the coffin was placed in a temporary vault. The following spring, dignitaries led by President Theodore Roosevelt, Ambassador Jean Jusserand from France, and Admiral George Dewey gathered in Dahlgren Hall to pay tribute to this great naval hero. At the end of the ceremony, the coffin was temporarily placed under the stairs in the rotunda of Bancroft Hall. Six years later, on January 26, 1913, the body was once again moved, this time to its final resting place in the crypt that had been designed to resemble Les Invalides, Napoleon's tomb in Paris. Tradition has it that while Jones's coffin remained in Bancroft, midshipmen were forbidden to whistle in the Hall out of respect for the father of the American Navy.

Another naval hero was laid to rest on January 20, 1917. On that cold and bitter day, the midshipmen traveled to Washington, D.C., to be the guard of honor at the funeral of Admiral George Dewey (Class of 1858), the ranking officer in the Navy. The last link between the old Navy and the new, Dewey began his career in the era of sailing ships and saw the dawn of the age of the aircraft carrier. Throughout his life, Admiral Dewey retained a special feeling for the midshipmen and frequently visited the Academy. It was he who laid the cornerstone of the new chapel, the Cathedral of the Navy, and he requested that when he died, midshipmen would be his only escort on the funeral route.

World War I and Its Aftermath

As the country edged toward entrance into World War I, the Academy was once again called on to supply ensigns for the burgeoning wartime fleet. Again, enrollment increased; graduations were held early; and, for the first time, reserve officers were trained at the Academy. Young men with a minimum of two years of college received a specialized three-month course in professional subjects under the leadership of Superintendent Edward W. Eberle (Class of 1885). Known as "ninety-day wonders," they supplemented the officers turned out by the Academy.

During the war, the major threat at sea came from German U-boats. With these submarines, Germany controlled the seas and seemed able to sink British ships at will. American shipping also suffered, and once the United States entered the war, it became necessary to transport huge numbers of men and supplies safely across the dangerous waters of the Atlantic. Rear Admiral William S. Sims (Class of 1880) developed a revolutionary strategy to counter U-boat attacks. It was his idea to surround troop transports and supply ships with destroyers and convoy them to England. Altogether, America sent two million doughboys to fight in France, and because of the convoy system, not one ship carrying them "over there" was sunk by German submarines. The famous slogan of the time summed it all up: "The Navy took 'em over and the Navy brought 'em back."

Although the American fleet did not engage in any sea battles, the Navy played an important role in wresting control of the seas from Germany. Working with the British and the French, the Americans helped to lay an antisubmarine minefield in the North Sea from the Orkneys to the coast of Norway. In addition, the Navy sent one of its aviation bombing squadrons to France and a battleship division to the British Grand Fleet. Five of the ships were assigned to the strategic naval base at Scapa Flow in the North Sea, the place where German crews were to scuttle their entire fleet after the war had ended. The youngest American commander at Scapa Flow was Captain Archibald H. Scales (Class of 1887), who was called to the Naval Academy as superintendent in February 1919 and would see the Academy through its transition back to peacetime status.

Scales found an Academy running smoothly although still recovering from the influenza epidemic that had swept the country. As of October 19, 1918, more than fifteen hundred midshipmen had come down with the flu, and eleven had died. In the diary he kept in his plebe year, William Sebald (Class of 1922), future diplomat and expert on Japan, described the epidemic's effect: midshipmen were quarantined within the Academy walls; football games and church parties were canceled; and hundreds of mids were hospitalized. Although the worst had passed by late fall, many of the young men remained in weakened condition until spring.

During Superintendent Scales's tenure, the nation's euphoria at winning the war began to turn to disillusionment. America had entered the Great War full of idealism, ready to fight the war to end all wars. President Woodrow Wilson was hailed in France as a conquering hero come to make the world safe for democracy. But the idealistic hopes for a peaceful world were shattered by the infighting among the victorious Allies and demands for vengeance. The American people, disheartened, again felt betrayed by the corrupt Old World. Isolationist and antimilitary sentiment prevailed, and the Naval Academy felt the repercussions. It was clear that the regiment, which had tripled in size to meet wartime needs, would be greatly reduced. Appropriations for the Academy would also suffer, and the military profession was no longer as highly esteemed as it had been during the war.

One way in which lowered morale manifested itself at the Academy was in a resurgence of hazing. Because of a Congressional investigation into the problem in 1920, Superintendent Scales demanded that the first class sign a statement promising not to haze the plebes. When they refused to sign, he separated the plebes from the upperclassmen in Bancroft Hall and forbade any contact between them. This Segregation Incident infuriated the upperclassmen, who resented the loss of their traditional privileges, and troubled the plebes, who knew they would eventually suffer the wrath of the upperclassmen.

Hanson W. Baldwin (Class of 1924), the famous war correspondent and military affairs editor of the *New York Times*, was a plebe during this crisis. He was called before an inquiry board and ordered to identify mids involved in hazing. Though young, naive, and terrified, he refused to name names and expected to be dismissed for deliberate disobedience of orders. While spared the ultimate punishment, he was given one hundred demerits, which not only drastically lowered his class standing but also denied him what few privileges he had as a plebe. He felt vindicated, however, when an upperclassman whispered "good show" when the demerits were read out. The high number proved that he had not betrayed anyone to the authorities. When it became clear that the superintendent would not back down, the first class signed the pledge, and the segregation crisis ended.

Superintendent Scales was replaced by Rear Admiral Henry B. Wilson (Class of 1881), who, according to Hanson Baldwin, was universally respected and admired by the midshipmen for his great sense of justice and fairness. He always called them "young gentlemen" and expected them to live up to the name. They in turn called him "Uncle Henry" and praised him for bringing back discipline and pride to the Academy. He upgraded the curriculum, increased entrance requirements, and attempted to eliminate hazing by awarding privileges to each class by seniority.

The Navy's first submarine, the USS Holland, was based at the Naval Academy from 1900 to 1905.

Along with his successors, Rear Admiral Louis M. Nulton (Class of 1889) and Rear Admiral Samuel S. Robison (Class of 1888), Superintendent Wilson had to deal with the repercussions of the Washington Conference of November 1921, which limited naval armaments. The agreement called for the United States to suspend construction of new ships for ten years and, in addition, to destroy almost thirty existing ships. As a result of the downsizing, many midshipmen were encouraged at graduation to apply for reserve commissions or to resign their commissions altogether. On the positive side, at this time the Academy was granted accreditation by the Association of American Universities and was authorized to grant bachelor of science degrees to its graduates.

The 1930s were difficult years for the country and the world at large. The collapse of the financial markets and the ensuing unemployment brought about a global depression, the effects of which were felt at the Academy. Superintendent Thomas C. Hart (Class of 1897), faced with major budgetary cutbacks, had to reevaluate the program and reduce staff. Nevertheless, he ran the Academy efficiently with greatly diminished funds and, at the same time, succeeded in teaching the midshipmen to manage their funds as well. Although technically against regulations, for years many new graduates had entered the fleet with large debts that they had incurred during their four years in Annapolis. Under Hart, they left the Academy with an average of one thousand dollars in savings.

Budgetary cutbacks imposed on the Navy had an especially deleterious effect on the Class of 1933. Only one semester away from graduation, they learned that only the top half of the class would receive commissions; the rest would be honorably discharged. Having worked so hard for four years, they suddenly found themselves about to be released into civilian life, with its dim job prospects. Some found places in the Army Air Corps. Fortunately for many of the others, Congress reversed the ruling the following year, and they were offered their commissions. Those who accepted were known as the Class of 1933 B; the Army aviators who returned to the Navy were designated the Class of 1933 C and were called "Army Aces"; and those who rejoined to fight in World War II were called the Class of 1933 D. Despite the difficulties many had securing their commissions, 11 percent of the Class of 1933 eventually made flag rank.

World War II, Academy Men at the Helm

As the decade drew to a close, President Franklin D. Roosevelt became increasingly alarmed at the threat of a rearmed Germany and its belligerence toward its neighbors. At Roosevelt's urging, Congress passed an act in May 1937 permitting the United States to sell goods to European nations provided that they paid in cash and transported the materials in their own ships. This "cash and carry" policy was intended to aid Britain and France. With the fall of Paris on June 14, 1940, Roosevelt signed the naval expansion bill, and shortly thereafter, Congress appropriated four billion dollars—an amount unprecedented in peacetime—to build a "two-ocean navy."

In the fall of 1940, the country went even further. Roosevelt promised "all aid short of war" to Great Britain, which was standing alone against Germany, and by executive order exchanged fifty old American destroyers for eight British air and naval bases. As the president told the American people in a December fireside chat, the United States "must be the great arsenal of democracy." With the passage of "An Act to Promote the Defense of the United States"—better known as Lend-Lease—the United States did become Britain's arsenal, providing fifty billion dollars' worth of supplies

Midshipmen stroll with their ladies down tree-lined Lovers Lane at the turn of the century.

Annapolis 5

Following the April 24, 1906 ceremony in the Armory, dignitaries including President Theodore Roosevelt, French Ambassador Jusserand, Admiral of the Navy George Dewey (Class of 1858) and General Horace Porter escort the coffin of John Paul Jones to its temporary resting place in the newly constructed Bancroft Hall.

and matériel. And when Roosevelt ordered American ships to "shoot on sight" German submarines, the country essentially entered an undeclared naval war.

Once again world events prompted changes at the Academy. With the country engaged in a substantial military buildup—including America's first peacetime draft—large numbers of officers were needed to staff the two-ocean Navy. The Class of 1941 was graduated early, and a three-year curriculum replaced the normal four-year program beginning with the plebes of 1940. Just as in World War I, reservists were trained at the Academy. All told, the Academy prepared thousands of young men to fight on the Atlantic and Pacific.

On December 7, 1941, Superintendent Russell Willson (Class of 1906) and his wife were hosting a reception in their home for the football team to celebrate its 14-6 victory over Army a week earlier. As football star Captain William S. "Barnacle Bill" Busik (Class of 1943) recalls, "Superintendent Willson was called away to the telephone. He walked up the stairs, to the family's living quarters. After the phone call he came down the steps, called us all into a central area of the house and said, 'Gentlemen, we are at war. We've been bombed at Pearl Harbor by the Japanese. Return to your quarters.'" Over in Smoke Hall, other midshipmen were attending a dance. Guards entered, reported the attack, and ushered the visiting young ladies off the Academy grounds. The gates were already secured by armed Jimmy-Legs, and according to Captain Busik, the mates on deck in Bancroft were armed as well. "The scariest thing about the whole war was seeing fellow mids armed."

More than ever before, World War II demonstrated to the nation the leadership and capabilities of Academy men. On December 20, 1941, Admiral Ernest J. King (Class of 1901) was named commander in chief of the United States fleet. In the "short of war" phase, King had overseen the neutrality patrols, and in the early months of 1942, it was his task to counter the U-boat offensive directed against North America's East Coast. Ships had been attacked just a few miles off New York City, Virginia Beach, and the entrance to the Panama Canal. Eventually, the use of small escort vessels for the coast and an interlocking convoy system with air support for open waters protected Allied shipping. In March 1942, Admiral King became Chief of Naval Operations (CNO) and coordinated all United States naval strength with the Allies.

Rear Admiral H. Kent Hewitt (Class of 1907) became a master of the amphibious landing. He commanded the Western Naval Task Force in the invasion of North Africa, the first amphibious operation launched an ocean away. Sailing from Hampton Roads in late October 1942, his force defeated the Vichy French fleet off Casablanca and before dawn on the morning of November 8 landed General George S. Patton's forces ashore. At Sicily in July 1943, the largest amphibious action of the war, Hewitt's forces once again landed Patton's Seventh Army, this time under the cover of darkness, using the new LST, LCT, and LCI beachcraft. All that Hewitt had learned in the African and Italian campaigns he put to use in his faultlessly executed landing on August 15, 1944, near Marseilles. This operation opened up supply routes and landed troops to aid in the final assault on Germany.

In the most celebrated amphibious landing of the war, Operation Overlord, six hundred warships and thousands of support vessels crossed the English Channel before dawn on June 6, 1944, and moved into position to begin the Allied invasion of Normandy. Rear Admiral Alan G. Kirk (Class of 1909) landed fifty-five thousand American troops on Omaha and Utah beaches and then bombarded German positions ashore. Never before had land and naval forces worked so successfully together to achieve such a difficult objective.

A Masqueraders production. Midshipmen theatrical groups have been a tradition at the Academy since the Spirits Club performed "The Lady of Lyons" shortly after the School's founding.

For all its success in the Atlantic, it was in the Pacific that the Navy faced its greatest challenge, and Academy men planned and executed the strategy. As Kenneth J. Hagan wrote in *This People's Navy*, the war was "fought by a small group of top commanders, about a dozen in all. They had known each other at the Naval Academy between 1901 and 1905 and were professionally and personally dedicated to one another. Nimitz emerged as *primus inter pares* of this elite cadre. . . ." Chester W. Nimitz (Class of 1905) was named commander in chief of the Pacific Fleet on December 17, 1941. Under his command, the fleet waged stunningly successful campaigns against the overpowering naval force of the Empire of Japan.

Immediately after Pearl Harbor, the Japanese began a relentless push toward domination of the Pacific. Within weeks, they had taken Siam (Thailand), Singapore, Guam, the Gilbert Islands, Hong Kong, and Wake Island. The Philippines, essential to both Japanese and American strategy in the Pacific, fell to Japan with the surrender of Corregidor in the spring of 1942. The Japanese drove relentlessly on until the battles of the Coral Sea and Midway finally halted them. In the Coral Sea, the aircraft carriers *Lexington* and *Yorktown*, commanded by Rear Admiral Frank Jack Fletcher (Class of 1906), fought the enemy in the first carrier battle in naval history. Though neither side won a decisive victory, the encounter thwarted the Japanese plan to take Port Moresby and move on to Australia.

The Battle of Midway was the crucial turning point of the war in the Pacific. Admiral Yamamoto, the commander of Japan's combined fleet, needed Midway as a base for launching attacks to deliver the death blow to Pearl Harbor. Nimitz, anticipating Yamamoto's move, strengthened the air defense at Midway and ordered Rear Admiral Raymond A. Spruance (Class of 1907) to join Admiral Fletcher northeast of the island. The Americans, with only three aircraft carriers and several cruisers and destroyers, were greatly outnumbered by the Japanese force of more than two hundred ships, including eight carriers and eleven battleships. After executing a devastating aerial attack on Midway, the Japanese carrier force commander, Admiral Nagumo, learned that the American carriers were fast approaching. In what turned out to be a grave tactical error, he ordered his planes unloaded and rearmed to strike the American ships. In the midst of the rearming, with most of the guns out of commission, American dive bombers attacked and sank half his carriers, forcing him to retreat. Nimitz's strategy had dealt the Imperial Navy its first defeat in the twentieth century and set the stage for America to go on the offensive in the Pacific.

In order to take the war to the home islands of Japan, the United States embarked on what turned out to be a three-year, island-by-island campaign. It began with the fight for the strategic airstrip on Guadalcanal in the Solomon Islands. The First Marine Division landed there on August 7, 1942, and took Henderson Field. For three bloody months, the Marines repelled repeated enemy attacks without supplies or reinforcements. Aid finally arrived after the South Pacific Force, under the command of Vice Admiral William F. "Bull" Halsey (Class of 1904), won the naval battle of Guadalcanal in mid-November. In that battle, Rear Admiral Willis A. Lee (Class of 1908) successfully used radar in a night attack to sink the Japanese battleship *Kirishima*. Three more months of battles ensued, employing air, naval, and ground forces. On February 9, 1943, the Japanese evacuated Guadalcanal, giving the world notice that this seemingly invulnerable foe could be beaten.

After Guadalcanal, American strategy called for action in both the south and central Pacific. Admiral Halsey was to secure the rest of the Bismarck Archipelago and neutralize the Japanese stronghold of Rabaul on New Britain. In the course of this action, Captain Arleigh A. Burke (Class of 1923), a future Chief of Naval Operations, sank three of five Japanese destroyers as they attempted to reinforce an island position.

Meanwhile, in the central Pacific, Admiral Nimitz's forces were fighting for control of the Gilbert and Marshall Islands in the first major

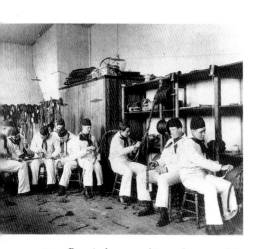

Practical seamanship at the turn of the century: mids learn knotting and splicing.

amphibious actions in the Pacific. The Fifth Fleet, commanded by Rear Admiral Spruance and Rear Admiral Richmond Kelly Turner (Class of 1908), landed Marines on the small island of Tarawa in the Gilberts. At a tremendous cost—913 Marines dead and more than twice that number wounded—the island was taken and became a base for launching air attacks on the Marshalls. Early in 1944, Rear Admirals Turner and Harry W. Hill (Class of 1911), Academy superintendent from 1950 to 1952, directed the amphibious action against the Japanese headquarters at Kwajalein in the Marshalls. They succeeded without losing a single American ship and suffered few casualties. Much of the credit for the low number of casualties belongs to Rear Admiral Marc Mitscher (Class of 1910), who so ably used the carriers under his command to destroy Japanese aircraft in the weeks preceding the landings.

Spruance's next objective was to provide protection for the American land forces on the Mariana Islands. Marines, landed by Admiral Turner on June 15, encountered heavy resistance on the island of Saipan and later on Tinian and Guam. More than twenty-five thousand Americans were killed, wounded, or missing in action on the Marianas, while the Japanese reported forty-five thousand killed and thousands more wounded. Victory would not have been possible without Spruance's Fifth Fleet. Not only did he guard the approach by sea, but his carriers sent up Hellcat fighters, which downed 345 enemy planes in the Battle of the Philippine Sea and virtually destroyed Japanese air power. The Marianas were secured as a base for launching air attacks against the Japanese home islands, fourteen hundred miles away.

Graduation exercises in the Armory, Dahlgren Hall, in 1923. Among the 412 graduates was future CNO Arleigh A. "31-Knot" Burke.

The stage was now set to liberate the Philippines and redeem General Douglas MacArthur's pledge to return. The attack on the Philippine island Leyte, originally set for December 20, 1944, was moved up two months at the insistence of Admiral Halsey, who was known for his aggressiveness in battle. On October 20, Vice Admiral Thomas C. Kincaid's (Class of 1908) Seventh Fleet landed MacArthur's troops. In a last-ditch effort, Japan decided to send its entire navy against the American ships protecting the troops on Leyte. Dividing their fleet into three parts, the Japanese engaged the Americans in three separate battles on October 25. Rear Admiral Jesse Oldendorf (Class of 1909) defeated the Southern Force at Surigao Strait. Admiral Halsey was lured away by the Northern Force, leaving Rear Admiral Clifton Sprague's (Class of 1918) small carrier group to withstand the full brunt of the Center Force. With great courage and skill, Sprague defeated the overpowering Japanese fleet of four battleships, eight cruisers, and ten destroyers. Meanwhile, Admiral Mitscher's planes sank the four carriers of the Northern Force. The sea battles, known together as the Battle of Leyte Gulf, effectively disabled Japan's naval power for the rest of the war.

In February 1945, the Marines began the heroic effort to take Iwo Jima. Admiral Nimitz had decided on Iwo Jima as a base for fighter planes that would protect the Superfortress aircraft that were bombing Tokyo from the Marianas. Admiral Turner's Fifth Fleet landed the Marines on the nineteenth, and after four weeks of savage fighting, they took the island at a cost of more than sixty-eight hundred Americans dead and twenty-one thousand wounded.

Loading drill, five-inch guns, 1925.

In preparation for the invasion of Japan, American forces advanced toward Okinawa. Once again, Admiral Spruance, along with Admirals Turner and Mitscher, planned the attack and provided naval cover for the landings. Although the Japanese Navy had been rendered powerless at Leyte, the American fleet nevertheless suffered enormous losses. Kamikaze pilots on suicide missions inflicted severe damage on seven carriers and sank many other ships. All told, in this action more than thirty ships were lost and twice that number totally disabled. Moreover, fighting on land took a terrible toll on the Marines and soldiers. But Okinawa provided a base for the forays against the Japanese coast by Admiral John S. McCain's (Class of 1906) carrier task force and was deemed essential for the planned Allied invasion of Japan.

However, all-out invasion proved unnecessary. The horror of the first atomic bombs dropped on Hiroshima and Nagasaki convinced the Japanese to capitulate. On September 2, 1945, General Douglas MacArthur received the Japanese surrender on the deck of Admiral Halsey's flagship *Missouri* in Tokyo Bay. Fleet Admiral Nimitz was aboard and signed the documents as commander in chief of the Pacific Fleet.

Never before in the history of the world had a war been fought on such a massive scale. The Navy found it a formidable task to coordinate amphibious landings, submarine warfare, naval aviation, battleships, destroyers, cruisers, and carriers across two oceans and over thousands of miles. With men like Admirals King and Nimitz to plan operations and Admirals Halsey and Spruance to execute them, the Naval Academy provided the leadership that won the war in the Atlantic and the Pacific. As James V. Forrestal, the nation's first Secretary of Defense, declared, "You couldn't have won without the codes of professional attainments of men who had gone to Annapolis . . . and who provided the foundation of professional skill which [gave us] the best and greatest fighting fleet the world has ever seen."

With news of victory over Japan, the Academy exploded in celebration. Mids rushed to T-Court and snake-danced around Tecumseh to the tunes of a hastily assembled midshipman band. From windows flung open in Bancroft, midshipmen tossed streamers and confetti on the crowd below. Victory signs painted on bedsheets were paraded through the Yard. Above the din, the Japanese Bell ran out continuously far into the night.

The Academy Celebrates Its Centennial

Just two months later, the Academy celebrated once again, and the attention of a grateful nation was focused on its centennial festivities. For a full week an air of excitement attended the parades, dances, and displays of warships and aircraft as the Academy remembered its first one hundred years.

The week began with a solemn service in the Chapel in memory of the 729 graduates who had given their lives for their country. Wednesday, October 10, was designated Centennial Day. It began with morning colors, and the ships in the harbor displayed the Stars and Stripes and ran multicolored flags from bow to stern. With elected officials, military heroes, an honor guard of West Point cadets, and other dignitaries in attendance, the brigade assembled in Tecumseh Court. At 10:51 A.M. the station guns fired a one-hundred-gun salute in honor of the Academy's one hundred years. At precisely 11:00 A.M., Superintendent Aubrey W. Fitch (Class of 1906) read Commander Franklin Buchanan's original address, which had been delivered on that very spot on October 10, 1845. Seven cadet captains from West Point then presented the helmsman's wheel from the battleship *Maine* to the brigade commander.

Later that day, the honor guard of cadets joined the brigade in a parade on Worden Field. Three platoons of midshipmen dressed in uniforms from 1845, 1870, and 1900 were the highlight of the review. Those representing 1845 wore blue jackets and straw hats; the midshipmen clothed in uniforms of 1870 had high collars with gold crossed anchors; and the ones wearing uniforms of 1900 sported rows of gold buttons and stripes to represent class years. At a costume ball held that night at nine o'clock, members of the historic platoons, still garbed in their period uniforms, appeared with their dates, attired in dresses of the same era. The other young ladies wore costumes of the nineteenth century. At midnight, eight bells sounded from the Japanese Bell, which had been moved to the balcony of Dahlgren Hall. The brigade sang "Navy Blue and Gold," and with the playing of "The Star-Spangled Banner," Centennial Day officially came to an end.

The final day of celebration, Saturday, October 13, centered on the Navy football game against Penn State. Squadrons of dive bombers flew over the Chapel dome and demonstrated battle formations for the fans in Thompson Stadium. They then formed an arrowhead enclosing the number 100, symbolizing the Centennial. During halftime, midshipmen carried the emblems of the state or territory from which they were appointed to create a colorful massing of flags. The football team ended the week with a resounding 28-0 triumph on the field.

The Centennial Celebration carried the euphoria of victory into the fall of 1945. But, as is usually the case, the aftermath of war brought a reexamination of the nation's needs for naval power. While the United States was committed to maintaining a strong and visible Navy because of the unstable world situation, it was difficult to convince the American people to support huge appropriations. Many ships were decommissioned; others were mothballed; and implementation of many wartime technological advances had to be postponed.

Nevertheless, the Academy could no longer provide all the officers for the fleet, and various plans were proposed to remedy the situation. Some advocated turning all the service academies into two-year postgraduate programs for college men. Others wanted to build additional academies, and still others wanted to consolidate all the academies into one. It was Rear Admiral James L. Holloway, Jr. (Class of 1919), who convinced Congress to retain the academies in their traditional state. On his recommendation, the Naval Reserve Officer Training Corps (NROTC) was established on college campuses to supply the additional officers needed for the fleet. During Admiral Holloway's years as superintendent from 1947 to 1950, he continued to advocate the four-year academy program and was instrumental in the plans to found a separate school for the Air Force.

The Korean War

With the surprise invasion by North Korean forces into South Korea on June 25, 1950, the United States joined with other members of the United Nations to turn back the Communist aggression. Because the United Nations' police action in Korea was limited in scope, the Academy had no need to increase the number of junior officers it supplied to the fleet. It was not necessary, therefore, to telescope the four-year program, graduate midshipmen early, or train reservists in the Yard. Academy men once again provided crucial leadership at the highest levels of command. Vice Admiral C.

Turner Joy (Class of 1916), the Commander, Naval Forces, Far East, worked with other United Nations commanders to secure control of Korean waters.

On land, however, the North Koreans pushed south unchecked for almost three months. On September 15, in a daring lightning raid planned by General Douglas MacArthur, United Nations' troops were landed at Inchon far behind enemy lines. This amphibious action, under the command of Rear Admiral Arthur Dewey Struble (Class of 1915), required precise, split-second timing because of the extreme tides, which varied up to thirty feet per day and could leave vessels stranded in mud flats. The Tenth Corps, which included the First Marine Division, captured Kimpo air field and recaptured the South Korean capital of Seoul. By the end of September, the North Korean Army was in retreat.

At this point MacArthur, anxious to bring the conflict to a swift conclusion, divided his army in two, making a grave tactical error. Vice Admiral Joy vehemently opposed the plan, but MacArthur overrode his objections. At the general's orders, the Navy transported X Corps to Wonsan, where they were to begin their march to join the Eighth Army at the Yalu River. However, MacArthur failed to foresee that the Chinese would send one hundred thousand troops across the border to aid the North Koreans. As Samuel Eliot Morison records, the Chinese "attacked each strung-out column on its exposed flank [and forced] a fighting retreat against attacks of vastly superior strength, through mountain passes and valleys, in bitter cold and deep snow." Miraculously, over one hundred thousand United Nations' troops made it back to Hungnam and were evacuated in a brilliantly planned action by the Navy.

By the end of March, the United Nations forces had retaken Seoul and had reestablished control up to the thirty-eighth parallel. Dissatisfied, MacArthur wanted to press on into North Korea and take the war into China as well. For refusing to accept a limited war and for resisting directives from his civilian superiors, MacArthur was relieved of his command by President Harry S Truman on April 11. Truce negotiations began on July 10, with the United Nations' delegation headed by Vice Admiral Joy, who carried on until he assumed the superintendency of the Naval Academy on August 4, 1952. Rear Admirals Arleigh A. Burke and R. E. Libbey (Class of 1922) also participated in the talks, which floundered over the issue of prisoner repatriation. The truce was finally signed on July 27, 1953.

The Korean War belied the prediction that the age of atomic weaponry would render the Navy obsolete as a fighting force. By blockading the coast, bombarding enemy positions, staging amphibious landings

The Chapel dome from the colonnade connecting Bancroft Hall with Dahlgren. Architect Ernest Flagg designed the Chapel as the focal point of the new Academy. When the elaborate "wedding cake" terra cotta on the dome deteriorated, it was replaced with copper in the late 1920s.

and evacuations, and providing carrier bases for aircraft and helicopters, the Navy proved essential to the war effort. The conflict showed that the threat of nuclear annihilation made it even more important for the United States to have numerous military options with which to fight future limited wars with conventional weapons.

Changing Times

Nevertheless, the nuclear age had dawned. Just as steam transformed the age of sail, nuclear power ushered in a new era for the Navy, and Academy men were at the forefront of the new technology. Perhaps the name most associated with the nuclear Navy is that of Admiral Hyman G. Rickover (Class of 1922). A pioneer in the Navy's use of nuclear energy, Rickover spearheaded the development of the USS *Nautilus*, the first nuclear-powered submarine. In addition, under the direction of Chief of Naval Operations Admiral Arleigh A. Burke, Rickover worked with Rear Admiral William F. Raborn, Jr. (Class of 1928) on the Polaris ballistic missile system. These nuclear missiles were designed to be launched from the Nautilus-class submarines. Admiral Rickover also took an active interest in recruiting top-notch junior officers to serve on nuclear-powered ships.

Among the first young officers to apply for a nuclear billet was Jimmy Carter (Class of 1947). His screening interview with then Captain Rickover made a lasting impression on the future president. As he recounted in his autobiography, *Why Not the Best?:*

> It was the first time I met Admiral Rickover, and we sat in a large room by ourselves for more than two hours, and he let me choose any subject I wished to discuss. Very carefully, I chose those about which I knew most at the time—current events, seamanship, music, literature, naval tactics, electronics, gunnery—and he began to ask me a series of questions of increasing difficulty. In each instance, he soon proved that I knew relatively little about the subject I had chosen.
>
> He always looked right into my eyes, and he never smiled. I was saturated with cold sweat.
>
> Finally, he asked me a question and I thought I could redeem myself. He said, "How did you stand in your class at the Naval Academy?" Since I had completed my sophomore year at Georgia Tech before entering Annapolis as a plebe, I had done very well, and I swelled my chest with pride and answered, "Sir, I stood fifty-ninth in

a class of 820!" I sat back to wait for the congratulations—which never came. Instead, the question: "Did you do your best?" I started to say, "Yes, sir," but I remembered who this was, and recalled several of the many times at the Academy when I could have learned more about our allies, our enemies, weapons, strategy, and so forth. I was just human. I finally gulped and said, "No, sir, I didn't *always* do my best."

He looked at me for a long time, and then turned his chair around to end the interview. He asked one final question, which I have never been able to forget—or to answer. He said, "Why not?"

In response to the postwar technological advances, the Academy reevaluated its curriculum. Beginning in September 1959, midshipmen were allowed to validate (place out of) core courses, giving them time for more advanced upper-level courses and electives. The old lockstep curriculum became a thing of the past. And to emphasize the importance of academics, a civilian dean was appointed in 1964 for the first time in the Academy's history. In spite of the fears that the professional aspects of the curriculum would be slighted, Dean A. Bernard Drought won the complete respect of the commandant and executive department.

In this period, Academy facilities were updated as well. Building projects of the 1950s included wings added to Bancroft Hall, the construction of Halsey Field House, and the extension of the athletic fields by means of landfill. Navy–Marine Corps Memorial Stadium, dedicated on September 26, 1959, was built with contributions from the Athletic Association and alumni. But even with these additions, facilities were still inadequate. In June 1963, the architects at John Carl Warnecke and Associates began to draw up a master plan rivaled in scope only by Flagg's plan at the turn of the century. The next decade saw the additions of Michelson, Chauvenet, Rickover, and Ricketts halls and Nimitz Library and the renovation of other buildings.

The civil rights movement sweeping the country had a great effect on the Academy in the 1960s. Only five blacks had entered the Academy before World War II, and none had stayed for more than one year. The first to graduate was Wesley A. Brown, appointed by Representative Adam Clayton Powell of New York. He came to the Academy in 1945 and was graduated and commissioned with his class in 1949. Still, few blacks chose the Academy in the postwar years, and the Navy decided to seek out qualified African-American applicants. In 1966, the Candidate Guidance Office undertook a special recruitment program assisted by an advisory group of six black midshipmen. This group included the first two African-Americans to

Planning the February 1945 invasion of Iwo Jima are, left to right, Rear Admiral W. H. P. Bloudy; future USNA Superintendent Rear Admiral Harry W. Hill (Class of 1911); Lieutenant General Holland M. Smith; and Vice Admiral Richmond Kelly Turner (Class of 1908).

serve as president of their respective classes—Charles F. Bolden, Jr. (Class of 1968), who became a Marine and entered NASA's astronaut program, and Anthony J. Watson (Class of 1970), who later served at the Academy as deputy commandant and has since been promoted to flag rank. The efforts of the Candidate Guidance Office, along with BOOST (the program to Broaden Opportunity for Officer Selection and Training) and NAPS (the Naval Academy Preparatory School), raised minority enrollments so that by 1976, two hundred African-Americans were taking part in all aspects of Academy life. That year Mason C. Reddix, Jr. (Class of 1976), was appointed the first black brigade commander, the highest ranking midshipman. Today, 7 percent of midshipmen are African-Americans.

The civil rights movement was only one of many revolutions that shook the country during the 1960s. America's youth rebelled against all forms of accepted social standards, and the military establishment became a prime target. Massive demonstrations took issue with the country's involvement in Vietnam, and college campuses erupted in protest marcies, sit-ins, and draft-card burnings. Many Americans questioned the need for an academy to educate an elite body of professional Navy and Marine Corps officers. Between 1965 and 1970, applications for admission to the Academy declined. It was a hard time for midshipmen. They found themselves in fundamental disagreement with many of their peers, who subjected them to jeers and derision. They were often harassed even in civilian dress because of their short hair and military bearing. Nevertheless, many dedicated young men chose the unpopular course, and they, along with other Academy graduates, displayed outstanding leadership and extraordinary heroism in Vietnam.

The War in Vietnam

The United States entered the conflict in Indochina in an attempt to prevent a Communist takeover of South Vietnam. According to the then-popular "domino theory," if Vietnam fell, the other countries in Southeast Asia would topple in quick succession like a row of dominoes. Beginning with the Eisenhower administration, military advisors were sent to aid the South Vietnamese government, and during the Kennedy years, the number increased to more than sixteen thousand. When Lyndon Johnson assumed the presidency, he expanded the American commitment. He used the Gulf of Tonkin incident in August 1964 as justification for ordering air strikes against naval installations in North Vietnam. Once Congress passed the Tonkin Gulf Resolution, Johnson considered that he had a mandate to escalate the conflict without a direct declaration of war, and in 1965, Marines, the first American ground combat troops, were landed at Da Nang.

Just as in the limited conflict in Korea, the Navy was called on to control the seas, land troops, and provide fire cover and air bombardment. But in Vietnam, the Navy had an additional task. Because the enemy was waging a guerrilla war, the Navy had to secure the inland waterways, which provided infiltration routes for men and supplies from the north. According to Kenneth J. Hagan in *This People's Navy*, these in-country operations took an enormous toll. Beginning with Operation Game Warden in the Mekong Delta in 1966 and continuing through Sea Lords, instituted by Vice Admiral Elmo R. Zumwalt, Jr. (Class of 1943), in 1968, Navy men intercepted and boarded hundreds of thousands of Vietnamese small craft, landed ground forces, and provided covering fire for troops on the rivers' shores. The Navy suffered more casualties in Sea Lords than in any other surface operation during the war.

It was a bloody conflict on the ground as well, especially for the Marines. All told, they lost twice as many men as any of the other services and suffered more casualties than they had in World War II. They faced ambushes by a seemingly invisible enemy that could strike with deadly force and fade back into the jungle. No territory was safe. Even "friendly" villages might harbor Viet Cong, who moved through the countryside with ease. Marines were always on the front line, whether on reconnaissance missions or in pitched battle. Even with President Nixon's policy of "Vietnamization"—the transfer of responsibility for direct combat to the South Vietnamese Army—Marines continued to perform heroically, fighting alongside the South Vietnamese forces.

In 1972, Captain John W. Ripley (Class of 1962) performed one of the single most courageous acts of the war. He was serving as an advisor to the Third Vietnamese Marine Battalion during the Easter offensive. Thirty thousand North Vietnamese troops were preparing to cross the Dong Ha bridge and move on the provincial capital in Quang Tri and the ancient capital city of Hue. If the bridge could be destroyed, the enemy advance would be halted. Captain Ripley, using his Force Reconnaissance training, single-handedly placed over five hundred pounds of explosives under the bridge while under two hours of continuous fire from tanks and infantry troops. He made twelve trips, swinging hand over hand to position the charges. The bridge was demolished, stranding the enemy on the other side of the river. For this act of valor, Captain Ripley earned the Navy Cross.

Acts of heroism by Academy men were not confined to the battlefield

Fleet Admiral Chester W. Nimitz (Class of 1905) signs the instrument of Japanese surrender aboard the USS Missouri *on September 2, 1945. Behind Admiral Nimitz are, left to right, General Douglas MacArthur, Admiral William F. "Bull" Halsey (Class of 1904), and Rear Admiral Forrest P. Sherman (Class of 1918). The table on which the surrender was signed came from the ship's mess and is now part of the USNA Museum collection.*

Because of wartime restrictions, the 1942 Army-Navy game was played at the Naval Academy's Thompson Field. President Franklin D. Roosevelt ordered half of the Regiment of Midshipmen to learn Army songs and to cheer for West Point since the Corps of Cadets could not travel to Annapolis.

Navy landing craft disgorge supplies onto the shores of Iwo Jima just a few hours after Marines had established a beachhead on the island.

but occurred in the prisoner-of-war camps as well. Many naval aviators who had been downed on reconnaissance and bombing missions suffered greatly at the hands of their captors in the Hoa Lo prison, known facetiously as the Hanoi Hilton. Through torture and isolation, the North Vietnamese attempted to demoralize individual prisoners and force them to denounce the war and the American government.

Prisoners quickly learned that they had to develop a disciplined regimen of physical and mental exercise. Because they were held in individual cells and forbidden to speak, each was left to his own resources. Vice Admiral William P. Lawrence (Class of 1951), a POW for almost six years, forced himself to do calisthenics daily. Even more important were the mental activities he devised for himself. He filled many hours reliving his entire life, starting with his earliest memories. He would try to recall the name of every person in his grade school classes and review every incident of his life until he was shot down. He taught himself how to calculate compound interest and did elaborate problems in his head. During one especially harrowing period, he spent days composing a poem in perfect iambic pentameter. "O Tennessee, My Tennessee" later became the official poem of his home state.

In order to counter the captors' demoralizing tactics, the prisoners set up a military organization complete with a chain of command. The senior naval officer was Captain James B. Stockdale (Class of 1947), held as prisoner of war for seven-and-a-half years. Realizing the importance of contact between the captives, he was actively involved in keeping open the covert communications system throughout the camp. Using an elaborate tap code, in which words were tapped out letter by letter on cell walls, Stockdale and others passed on vital information. Because communication brought unity to the prisoners and helped them to resist attempts to exploit them, the North Vietnamese severely punished anyone caught transmitting messages.

Many times Captain Stockdale was singled out for especially brutal treatment, because of both his status and his acts of defiance. For one particular show of courage, he was awarded the Medal of Honor. Fearing a round of retaliation against all the prisoners, Captain Stockdale on September 4, 1969, "deliberately inflicted a near-mortal wound to his person in order to convince his captors of his willingness to give up his life rather than capitulate." His valiant stand not only prevented the planned purge but caused the North Vietnamese to reduce considerably their reliance on torture.

Both Vice Admirals Stockdale and Lawrence give much credit to their Naval Academy training for their survival and ability to lead men under such adverse conditions. The discipline, physical and mental stamina, commitment to their men, and loyalty to the United States engendered by the Academy program stood them in good stead throughout their ordeal. They found, as Admiral Thomas H. Moorer (Class of 1933), Chief of Naval Operations from 1967 to 1970, noted, that the basic fundamentals of leadership under stress that were taught at the Academy, beginning with plebe year, allowed them to react quickly to combat conditions and to instill the cohesion so vital to a military unit. In this, America's longest war, Academy training once again proved its worth wherever Academy men fought their battles.

The Modern Academy

Vice Admiral William P. Mack (Class of 1937), who became superintendent in June 1972, symbolized the nation's transition from wartime to peacetime. Seven days before he assumed command of the Academy, he was under fire on his flagship just off the coast of Vietnam. In the fleet, he had observed that midshipmen did not share the same depth of knowledge of professional subjects. To remedy this situation, he developed a professional competency objectives program in which first classmen were instructed in professional subjects and had to pass an examination on the material in order to graduate. Response to the program was so favorable in the fleet that it became a CNO requirement not only at the Academy but for reserve officer and officer candidate training as well.

Admiral Kinnaird R. McKee (Class of 1951), who took over from Admiral Mack, faced an enormous challenge. In 1976, Congress enacted legislation permitting women for the first time to enroll at the Academy. For years, women had served successfully in the fleet. The Navy Nurse Corps was founded in 1908, and twenty nurses reported for duty that October. During World War II, WAVES (Women Accepted for Voluntary Emergency Service) played a significant role under the direction of Mildred H. McAfee, the first woman naval officer. After the war, most returned to civilian life, although some remained in the service. However, they had limited opportunities and saw sea duty only aboard hospital ships until 1978, when other ships were opened to them. Six years later, women gained entry to operational air reconnaissance squadrons, and by the 1990s, women were commanding ships, squadrons, and naval stations and had been selected for astronaut training.

Despite women's successful service in the fleet, their admission to the Academy was viewed as revolutionary. Many felt that the spartan conditions and rigorous training were not suitable for them. Others cited the combat exclusion law, which prohibited women from combat billets. They questioned the propriety of educating women for positions they would not be allowed to hold. However, as Vice Admiral Lawrence, superintendent from 1978 to 1981, commented, "The Naval Academy is one of the prime sources of career-oriented professional officers. In view of the important role of women in the Navy, it is only logical and proper that the Naval Academy graduate women officers."

The first female midshipmen, sworn in on July 9, 1976, faced the same demanding program as their male counterparts. With the exception of minor adjustments to physical requirements, women midshipmen participated fully in every aspect of Academy life—professional, academic, and physical. As Superintendent McKee reported to the Board of Visitors at the end of that first year, the women's performance in all areas of midshipman life was remarkably strong. As the first women progressed through their four years at the Academy, they assumed leadership positions alongside the men in the midshipman chain of command.

Today, women make up 10 percent of the brigade, and more and more are filling important leadership positions. In 1991, for the first time in the history of the Academy, a woman, Juliane Gallina (Class of 1992), was selected as brigade commander. Increasing numbers of women are being assigned as company officers and faculty members, providing role models and serving as mentors for women midshipmen. With the lifting of some of the combat exclusions, women can take advantage of expanded opportunities for service in the fleet as well, and with more than two hundred thousand on active duty and one hundred and fifty thousand in the Reserves, women form an integral part of the modern Navy.

On March 31, 1992, Lieutenant Commander Wendy B. Lawrence (Class of 1981) was selected by the National Aeronautics and Space Administration (NASA) as the first female naval aviator to train as an astronaut. She joined the distinguished company of other Naval Academy graduates who were presently or had been in the space program. Indeed, both Alan B. Shepard, Jr. (Class of 1945) and Walter M. Schirra, Jr. (Class of 1946), were chosen as original Mercury Seven astronauts in 1959. Shepard became the first American in space on May 5, 1961, when he made a fifteen-minute suborbital flight in the *Freedom VII* capsule. Ten years later, when he commanded the Apollo XIV mission, he made two surface excursions on the moon.

Wally Schirra flew in all three of NASA's earliest manned space programs—Mercury, Gemini, and Apollo. Schirra and Thomas P. Stafford

Jubilant mids celebrate victory over Japan on August 14, 1945. In honor of V–J Day, the Superintendent declared a two-day holiday, and midshipmen rang the Japanese Bell, painted Tecumseh, and confettied T-Court.

(Class of 1952) in *Gemini VI* performed the first rendezvous in space, coming within one foot of *Gemini VII* manned by James A. Lovell, Jr. (Class of 1952) and USMA graduate Frank Borman. Outnumbering the West Pointer three to one, the Naval Academy alumni came prepared with a "Beat Army" banner which they displayed in space. All told, thirty-six graduates of the Naval Academy have been chosen for the space program, a greater number than from any other educational institution.

The 1980s saw an increase in patriotism throughout the country and a renewed appreciation for those serving in the military. Applications to the Naval Academy rose, and facilities were again expanded and improved. Lejeune Hall was opened in 1981, and Macdonough Hall and the Norman Scott Natatorium were renovated. Construction began on Alumni Hall, a new brigade activities center, which would finally provide a place where the entire brigade could assemble. Dedicated on October 4, 1991, it was funded jointly by the federal government and private donations. More than half of the thirty-million-dollar cost came from Naval Academy alumni, faculty, staff, friends, and supporters, and areas throughout the hall are named for alumni who have dedicated themselves to the nation's service.

When Iraq invaded Kuwait in August 1990, midshipmen closely followed events in the Persian Gulf. Throughout Desert Shield and Desert Storm, the Navy patrolled the waters of the Gulf and worked closely with the other services to establish air dominance. Midshipmen saw illustrated in dramatic fashion the lessons of strategy and tactics learned in the classroom. They themselves participated in the Fleet Sponsor Program, sending care packages to ships and Marine ground units on combat duty.

As the Academy prepares for the twenty-first century, its mission will continue to be the preparation of officers for the fleet. Recognizing that the demise of the Soviet Union has changed the balance of world power, the Navy will be called on to work closely with the other services, just as it did in Desert Storm. This interservice cooperation will require forces that can work as cohesive units throughout the world, and their leaders must be prepared to coordinate operations on land, sea, and air. These are the leaders the Academy must send forth to meet the challenges of the new century. Throughout its one-hundred-and-fifty-year history, the Naval Academy has always taken the best from its past and responded to the demands of the future. As Vice Admiral James F. Calvert (Class of 1943) observed, "The Academy must always be a changing institution if it is to meet its obligation to the Navy and the country . . . responsive to the new requirements of our time while remaining loyal to the best in our heritage."

A new class arrives to join the brigade of midshipmen. To the amusement of upperclassmen, some bring tennis racquets and other luxuries of civilian life—soon to be replaced by white works and stencil ink.

I–Day, 1976. Women prepare to enter the brigade of midshipmen for the first time in history.

Following pages: An American landing ship (LST) approaches the coast of North Africa. The amphibious landings of the Western Naval Task Force under the command of Rear Admiral H. Kent Hewitt (Class of 1907) set the stage for future successful operations in both the Atlantic and Pacific, including the most celebrated of all—the D–Day landings in Normandy in June 1944.

CHAPTER FOUR

I-DAY TO HERNDON:

The Longest Year

From Blue Springs, Missouri, and Clifton Forge, Virginia, from New York City and Los Angeles, from towns and cities throughout the land, they come to face the challenge of four arduous years at the Naval Academy. Induction Day—I-Day—has begun. As the line snakes around Alumni Hall, families surround these young men and women who just days before were carefree high school students. Academically and athletically at the top of their classes, they were celebrated in their home towns, and many had grand send-offs as they left for Annapolis. Now they are about to commit themselves to a rigorous, disciplined way of life far different from the life they have known.

Inside Alumni Hall, the transformation begins. Candidates are checked in, given name tags, alpha numbers, and company assignments. They leave their civilian baggage behind and rush from station to station. They have their vision tested and blood drawn. They are whisked before barbers who, in assembly-line fashion, shear one thousand heads before noon. They are fitted for uniforms and issued "white works" and "dixie cups." Stuffing their gear in their laundry bags, they run to the loading dock, where they are taught to stand in formation and salute before heading off to Bancroft Hall, their home for the next four years. In the unrelenting heat, squad leaders assemble the plebes and teach them to stow their gear, form up, march, and carry themselves in a military manner. Squads run through Bancroft, drop for push-ups, and shout out plebe rates.

At 1800 hours, the newly transformed plebes march by company into Tecumseh Court. As parents and friends look on, they take the Oath of Office and officially become midshipmen fourth class. So demanding and exhausting is the day that some actually fall asleep during the ceremony and others, already learning to make use of every moment, study their plebe bible, *Reef Points*. After a brief good-bye to their families, plebes reassemble for evening meal formation, close-order drill, and more instruction until lights out. And I-Day is just a harbinger of what is to come.

As rigorous as I-Day is, graduates who were inducted before the 1991 completion of Alumni Hall would claim their I-Day was even more demanding. With no building large enough for all the processing, plebes had to run from the oppressively hot Halsey Field House to various stations throughout the Yard. Everywhere they went, they had to haul their gear along with them, and, drenched with sweat, they barely had time to change into white works for the Oaths of Office ceremony.

In the history of the Academy, I-Day itself is relatively new. For years, there was no official day when candidates were inducted. They came in small groups throughout the summer, and they stayed in town while they were

The line snakes around Alumni Hall at the start of I–Day.

tested and screened at the Academy. Those who were accepted went to Memorial Hall to be sworn in and joined the plebe training in progress. Some failed and were turned away. Still others were encouraged to report back after correcting their deficiencies. One young man from Mississippi had passed all his tests but was underweight. Like others before him, he was instructed to return home and eat bananas and ice cream. Four weeks later he returned and was admitted to the Class of 1947.

No matter what form I-Day takes, it marks the transition from civilian to military life. No longer can plebes choose for themselves how they will dress, how they will speak, how they will spend their time. They have signed away control over their daily lives. In return, they have been accepted into the company of the men and women who have gone before them and have taken their first steps toward becoming officers in the United States Navy.

Plebe Summer

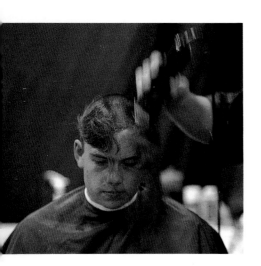

The transformation begins.

The frantic pace of I-Day continues throughout the six weeks of Plebe Summer. With the brigade away on summer cruises, the Yard is left to the plebes and the upperclassmen selected to train them. Plebe Summer is crucial. As one commandant said, it is the defining point in an Academy graduate's life. In a few short weeks, plebes are completely transformed. They learn to function in a military manner; they learn basic naval skills; they are pushed to their limits mentally and physically; and they do more than they ever thought they could.

Each day is a challenge. Reveille is at 0515, and by 0530 plebes have gathered on the athletic field for the Physical Education Program (PEP). Developed by Heinz Lenz in the early 1960s, this forty-five minutes of intense conditioning forever alters the meaning of the word *pep* for plebes. Set upon set of pull-ups, push-ups, and curl-ups follow jumping jacks, sit-ups, and explosive jumps. Plebes run along the seawall and engage in tug-of-war battles. Even the many varsity athletes struggle through the intense workouts. As Lenz, coach for twenty-five years, said, "We have to show the plebes from the very beginning that even if they are coming to us as All-American high school athletes, they are going to be challenged at the Naval Academy." Day by day they increase their strength, flexibility, and stamina, and by the end of the summer all are in top physical condition.

PEP is only the beginning. Physical demands continue throughout the day. Squads run from activity to activity, march in close-order drill, drop for push-ups when they have not mastered the information they were

assigned. Plebes never seem to have enough sleep, for they "rate their racks" only from 2200 to 0515. They become adept at snatching odd moments of sleep in unusual places—in the head, in their lockers, even in their closets on top of laundry bags. Being hot and tired feels normal to them, so the upper-class squad leaders are trained to look out for plebes who may be ill. One young man had strep throat with a fever of 102 degrees and did not even realize he was sick.

Mental demands are equally rigorous. Plebes must memorize and recite on demand the information in *Reef Points*, which ranges from Naval Academy customs, traditions, and ceremonies to the size, dimension, and purpose of ships in the modern Navy. They learn Naval Academy songs, cheers, and slang. Years later, graduates can still repeat verbatim,

At top, and above: Leaving their civilian baggage behind, candidates rush from station to station getting nametags, alpha numbers, and company assignments. They have their vision tested and blood drawn. Measured for uniforms, they are issued white works and dixie cups.

> Now these are the law of the Navy,
>   Unwritten and varied they be;
> And he who is wise will observe them,
>   Going down in his ship to the sea. . . .

They remember the name and hometown of each member of their Plebe Summer platoon. They know how many panes of glass are in the skylight of Bancroft Hall (489) and have a ready answer for "Why Didn't You Say Sir?" and "Why Is There No Excuse?" Some claim that no matter how hard they try, they cannot forget what they have learned as plebes. Football Hall of Famer Joe Bellino (Class of 1961) said, "I've forgotten the [football] signals, but I'll never forget those plebe routines."

Nor are plebes allowed to forget that they have joined the Navy. Bancroft Hall, which houses the Fourth Class regiment, is considered a ship, and plebes are expected to use proper naval terms. Walls are bulkheads; stairs are ladders; floors are decks. As in the fleet, plebes must stand watch and undergo room and personnel inspection. They learn how their gear must be stowed and how to wear and care for their uniforms. Mastering the details of each different uniform takes skill and concentration, and squad leaders will, at times, hold uniform races to teach speed and accuracy. Plebes are given three minutes, sometimes less, to change into PE gear and then told they have three minutes more to report back in their white works. Several other uniform changes happen in quick succession. Sometimes to ease tension, squad leaders order "white works Mickey Mouse" or "white works pirate." For Mickey Mouse, plebes appear with rolled black socks on their dixie cups; pirates appear with black sock eye patches.

91

First lessons: how to stand at attention and salute.

Plebes learn close-order drill and how to handle pistols and rifles. As the 1949 *Lucky Bag* noted, "Miss Springfield" became their constant companion. They march everywhere, and some begin to wonder whether they have joined the Army or the Navy. In the extraordinarily hot summer of 1990, the Regiment was marching on Hospital Point when one company commander could stand it no longer. He sprinted toward the Severn with his company running in formation behind him, and they all followed him into the river. Little did they realize that their plunge echoed an incident from the early days of the Academy. Many of the first midshipmen to come to the Naval School had already served at sea and strongly resisted marching. That was for "sojers," not for sailors. To make matters worse, the unpopular Professor Henry Lockwood, an 1836 West Point graduate who taught science at the Academy, had charge of infantry training. Mids ridiculed his stutter and were always trying to find ways to undermine his authority. Once during drill, Lockwood stuttered and could not call out the command to halt. The men marched right into the Severn, dragging their equipment behind them.

In addition to drills, plebes receive instruction in the basics of seamanship, navigation, and signaling. They all must learn to sail, which many consider the best part of their summer, a time when they can leave the tension of Bancroft Hall behind. No matter what level of expertise they bring with them—some come as competent sailors, others have never seen the water before—they all earn at least the "B" qualification at the end of the course and are designated senior crew members. As one officer in charge of plebe sailing said, "Because they're eventually going into the fleet, we want them to have a healthy respect as well as familiarity with the water. We teach . . . good seamanship and leadership."

Indeed, leadership is the keystone of the entire Academy program, and it sets the service academies apart from civilian universities. Leadership training begins on day one—I-Day. Since those who lead must first learn to follow, plebes are taught to respond to orders instantaneously. Their responses to upperclassmen are limited to "Yes, sir/ma'am," "No, sir/ma'am," "No excuse, sir/ma'am," and "I'll find out, sir/ma'am." They have sworn allegiance to an organization, and its interests must take priority over their own. When determining any course of action, they must think first of ship, then of shipmate, and only then of self.

Leadership is demonstrated by the upperclassmen who make up the Plebe Detail. Carefully chosen from the best of the brigade, they represent for many plebes their first real contact with the Naval Academy and the

United States Navy. No one ever forgets his Plebe Summer squad leaders. Plebe Detail leaders, told that their job is the most challenging, demanding, and rewarding one at the Naval Academy, work even harder than their charges. They are held responsible for their plebes' performance, while their words and actions have an unimaginable impact and remain with graduates throughout their careers.

The ultimate goal of Plebe Summer is to turn out leaders who will be able to function under pressure. Stress is constant. In addition to facing the heat, the exhaustion, the unrelenting pace, and the overwhelming amount of information to absorb, each plebe is singled out for correction many times during the summer. The squad usually suffers as well. "You're doing your push-ups because Mr. Smith felt it was time to take a breather." Or, "We'll go for a little run because Ms. Jones did not learn proper wardroom etiquette." Plebes learn that their actions have consequences and not just for themselves. The worst thing a plebe can do is to "bilge," or show up, a classmate. They learn that they must stand by and support one another. If not today, then tomorrow it will be their turn to be singled out, and they will need the help of their classmates to make it through.

As the 1962 *Lucky Bag* said of Plebe Summer, "The hectic routine left little time for such former pleasures as breathing." Commonplace things that were taken for granted just a few short weeks earlier take on new significance for plebes. To relieve stress, one squad leader held a limbo contest. The competition was great fun, but the best part for the plebes was hearing music again. They had no idea how much they had missed it. Other plebes had to find less conventional ways to let off steam. Vice Admiral Charles S. Minter, Jr. (Class of 1937), said that in the middle of one night during his Plebe Summer, a classmate put a fire hose down the voice tube and flooded the lower deck. The entire class was lined up by the duty officer, who appeared in his nightgown with his belt and sword strapped to his side. No one would admit to the deed, so the officer kept them standing at attention until three o'clock in the morning. It was not until his fortieth class reunion that the culprit acknowledged the prank, although his classmates will still not reveal his name.

Each class has its own memories. For generations of midshipmen, Plebe Summer meant the smell of stencil ink used to mark all their clothing and equipment. "The acrid fumes of stencil ink saturated our rooms and telltale smudges betrayed our first blundering efforts." For some, it was the smell and feel of stiff new white works. For others, it was the oppressive heat. In 1916, Orin Shepley Haskell (Class of 1920) wrote that it was so hot in

Chapel, he put his prayerbook behind his back to keep his uniform from sticking to the pew. He did not stick to the pew, but the red dye of the book stained his whites. Many graduates recall standing in noon formation with sweat pouring down their backs, soaking uniforms that were fresh only moments before. When midshipmen of today look back on their Plebe Summer, they remember filling and refilling their canteens, which they carried everywhere. One plebe summed it up, "Sweat, sweat, sweat. You never stop. You're never clean."

Plebe Summer seems endless, but after six weeks families arrive for Fourth Class Parents' Weekend. Begun in 1951 as an informal open house by Superintendent Harry W. Hill (Class of 1911), it has grown into a full weekend of special activities. Parents are amazed at the difference in their sons and daughters. These are not the same children they had left behind on I-Day. Rear Admiral Michael D. Haskins (Class of 1966) and his wife tell of seeing their daughter at Parents' Weekend. She walked right by her mother, who failed to recognize her, and surprised her father with a crisp salute.

Even those who, like Admiral Haskins, are graduates themselves and prepared for the change find themselves astonished. The plebes stand tall, move with an air of confidence, and seem to have matured overnight. They show an increased respect for their parents and an appreciation for the love and support of their families. Parents' Weekend is a celebration of all they have accomplished. The plebes feel intense pride at having made it through such a grueling experience—one that they would not have missed for the world, but one they would never want to repeat. As one plebe said, "Next year on I-Day, wherever in the world I am, I'm going to get down on my knees and give thanks that it's not me!"

There are several other hurdles before the academic year begins. The first is Black Sunday, the end of Parents' Weekend. As families depart, plebes return to Bancroft Hall, to be greeted by Christmas music blaring through open windows—the upperclassmen's way of reminding the plebes that they will not be going home until the holidays. The real shock, though, is the Return of the Brigade. As demanding as the summer was, it was geared entirely to the plebes and their training, with plebes outnumbering upperclassmen three to one. With all the midshipmen back at the Academy, the ratio is reversed, and the plebes learn their true place in the brigade. At the final formal parade of the summer, plebes are officially presented to the Brigade of Midshipmen, a significant event not just for the fourth classmen but also for the mids who have trained them. The Turnover Parade demon-

Standing watch in "Mother B."

strates that members of the Plebe Detail have successfully completed their task and have brought the fourth class up to the standards of the brigade. That evening, plebe year really begins. As the 1957 *Lucky Bag* put it, "Our peaceful little world crashed down around us," and Hell Night began.

Each company has its own special way to introduce plebes to upperclassmen on Hell Night. One company began the night in a darkened passageway with five minutes of utter silence. Another ran their plebes up and down the ladders, firing questions about uniforms, standing watch, and the chain of command. Still another posted formal invitations in the wardroom directing plebes to line up, nose against the bulkhead. With music from the movie *The Terminator* blasting and upperclassmen breathing down their necks, the command came, "Fourth class, meet your second class. About face!" Plebes found themselves nose to nose with screaming upperclassmen, and for two hours, they were quizzed on their rates and repeatedly dropped for push-ups. Upperclassmen flashed their room nameplates as the plebes desperately tried to memorize the names of members of their new unit.

Throughout the history of the Academy, the return of the upperclassmen from summer cruises has been an event both anticipated and dreaded by the plebes. William Sebald (Class of 1922) recorded in his diary the arrival of returning upperclassmen on battleships out near Kent Island. He and his fellow plebes immediately hid their socks and white service uniforms to prevent the upperclassmen from taking them. For Captain Stephen Jurika, Jr. (Class of 1933), the sight of battleships on the horizon signaled the end of summer. He watched as upperclassmen, bags slung over their shoulders, came ashore and sauntered with what "we thought a rather salty gait." They dropped their gear, grabbed some clothes, and departed for September leave. In present day, however, the brigade returns from summer cruises, and the academic year begins.

Every moment counts as candidates study Reef Points, *the plebe bible.*

Plebe Year

Plebe year is an intense nine-month trial during which plebes prove to themselves and to the Academy that they have earned the right to become full-fledged members of the brigade. Building on the foundation of the summer training, the program emphasizes leadership, teamwork, and the acquisition of professional knowledge. Plebes must also take a rigorous academic curriculum that includes courses in calculus, chemistry, history, naval science, and government. Plebe year is meant to be difficult, and approximate-

It is axiomatic that upon the strength of the keel depends the strength of the ship. Similarly, upon a Naval officer's "Plebe Year" depends much of his achievements in the Fleet.

Lucky Bag, 1947

ly 15 percent of the group does not make it through. But it molds those who stay the course into a cohesive, steadfast class and links them with all those who have gone before.

From reveille to taps, plebes never stop. In addition to a full schedule of classes, formations, and athletics, they have requirements specific to the fourth class. By breakfast formation, they must master daily rates, including the menus for breakfast, lunch, and dinner, a current news story, a sports story, and all stories dealing with the Navy. They must know the scores of the week's Army–Navy and Navy–Air Force games. Each week for professional development, they must learn and retain on a cumulative basis the "pro" topic of the week and present a report on it to their upperclassmen. Plebes are required to report to upperclassmen for "come-arounds" at various times throughout the week. At these sessions upperclassmen counsel, teach, or correct plebes.

Before morning and noon meal formations, a plebe from each company delivers the chow call, which includes the number of minutes until formation, the uniform required, the Officer of the Day, and the menu. Within Bancroft Hall, plebes must "chop" (march at double time) with "eyes in the boat" down the center of passageways and, while squaring corners, must sound off with a spirit phrase—"Go Navy, sir!" or "Beat Army, sir!" Plebes rate only authorized ladders and are prohibited from the Steerage and company wardrooms except on official business. They are also forbidden to have stereos, walkmen, or radios in their rooms. Plebes must report early to all formations and wear regulation uniforms except when in their rooms.

For years mealtimes were a special trial, an additional lesson in how to function under stress. In King Hall, plebes had to sit rigidly on the first few inches of their chairs with face front, head up, and feet flat on the floor. Unless given special permission, they could not speak, and if addressed by an upperclassman, they were required to stop eating and look directly at the questioner. At noon meal, they were quizzed on professional topics. As the 1937 *Lucky Bag* said, many felt that "plebes went to the mess hall merely to see that there was plenty of food for the first class, and to keep them amused."

In the early part of the century, plebes who could not answer questions from upperclassmen were sometimes ordered to eat under the table like dogs. Arthur Wilson (Class of 1931) found this no punishment at all. In fact, he preferred to eat under the table since there he did not have to brace up or face verbal abuse. He also tells of lighter moments at meals. Once in a

Forty-five minutes of intense conditioning—0530 to 0615—the Physical Education Program forever alters the meaning of the word "pep" for plebes.

while an upperclassman would suddenly shout, "Fire in the paint locker!" Plebes then jumped up and tied their napkins together to simulate a fire hose, using the "red-eye" (ketchup) bottle as the nozzle. They pretended to struggle to hold the hose steady under the tremendous pressure of the water, and if they gave a convincing performance they were released from restrictions—given "carry-on"—for the rest of the meal. In the 1940s, plebes could earn carry-on with a successful Sunday evening "Happy Hour" performance, a required five-minute entertainment to help dispel the gloom of the impending week. If their skits, songs, or antics pleased the upperclassmen, they were rewarded with carry-on.

Restrictions extend outside Bancroft Hall. Plebes may not sit anywhere in the Yard, although they may use any of the paths and walkways. This was not always the case. In other times, specific areas were off-limits, such as Smoke Park, Youngster Cutoff, and the walk inside the hedge in front of the Administration Building. A plebe in 1918 lamented, "By the time we poor mids ever get situated where we can take walks when, where and with whom we want to, we shall be so old that we shall have to ride."

Lovers Lane was also prohibited. This gravel path connecting Chauvenet Walk and Blake Road was not a secluded hideaway but rather a convenient route through the Yard. For years, midshipmen wondered at the blatant misnaming of this open walkway. The 1929–30 *Reef Points* stated that at one time it was bordered by a hedge which "was considered ill-placed and, hence, was removed. Let's get that landscape architect." So important was the right to use Lovers Lane that immediately following graduation, the new youngsters (third classmen) would snake-dance down the path and claim it for their own.

Plebes' social life has always been circumscribed. Historically, they have had few hours to spend at liberty in the Yard, even fewer to spend in the town of Annapolis, and no time outside city limits except on authorized occasions. Only when away from the Academy on leave have they been allowed to drive and to date, and they are not permitted to attend Academy balls. For years, however, part of their training as future officers and gentlemen included weekly dancing lessons in Memorial Hall taught by Professor Bell from Baltimore. Since there were no women at the Academy then, the plebes had to partner one another. At times, the instructor found it hard to keep order, but however much the plebes ridiculed him, they did learn to dance to his count of "One, two, three. . . . Boom, drip, drip; Boom, drip, drip." At the hops themselves, plebes could only look on from the balcony.

Attention to detail: they shine their shoes to mirror brightness.

"The hectic routine left little time for such former pleasures as breathing."
Lucky Bag, *1962*

It was one of their duties to rate the beauty of the upperclassmen's dates and decide which mid should later be awarded the brick for bringing the least attractive girl.

For plebes, the restrictions, rules, and regulations seem never-ending. As mids are fond of observing, "The Academy takes away all your God-given rights and returns them to you one by one as privileges." Not surprisingly, they do not succeed at doing everything perfectly at all times, and upperclassmen are ever ready to correct infractions. Through the years, the penalties exacted have ranged from the humorous to the cruel. In the 1870s, plebes had to mimic gorillas, bears, and other animals while acting out amusing poems. At the turn of the century, they often had to recite inane stories in the wardroom or sing their laundry lists to the tune of "Yankee Doodle." During his plebe year, war correspondent Hanson Baldwin (Class of 1924) was made to sing "Anchor's Aweigh" while standing on his head under the shower. In more recent times, Lieutenant Colonel Oliver L. North (Class of 1968) was sent out on the traditional nighttime "recon" to polish the brass balls of the statue of Bill the Goat.

Many demands were a good deal less humorous—at least to the plebes involved. Sometimes they were told to balance stacks of books on their outstretched arms or to hold other extreme positions for long periods of time. When ordered to "sit on the little green bench," they pressed their backs to the wall and "sat" a few inches off the floor. Upperclassmen liked to play a game known as cuckoo. A plebe, hidden under his study table, had to stick his head out and say "cuckoo." He then tried to get back before the upperclassman could swat him. Another favorite was making the fourth classmen drink a "plebe cocktail"—a mixture of all the sauces, seasonings, vinegars, and relishes on the table.

Sometimes, upperclassmen used their power to persecute a plebe they disliked. During his plebe year, Vice Admiral William R. Smedberg III (Class of 1926) spent Christmas leave in Washington, D.C. Coming from a formal party dressed in tuxedos, he and his friends went to a hamburger stand owned by the father of a first classman. The upperclassman was embarrassed and furious at the role reversal as he served the plebes, and back at the Academy, he put Smedberg on report for a trumped-up charge. The circumstances surrounding the allegation were so farfetched that the commandant eventually dismissed it, but not before Smedberg had endured great anxiety and trouble.

At times, physical punishments got out of hand. Plebes have been beaten with broom handles, coat hangers, curtain rods, and hairbrushes.

They were forced to do push-ups and deep knee bends until they dropped. A few plebes even died of excessive hazing. Periodically, Congressional investigations were held into the matter. As a result of one in 1920, Superintendent Archibald H. Scales (Class of 1887) segregated the entire fourth class on the upper floors of Bancroft Hall. First classmen were made to stand guard on the stairs with fixed bayonets. Only when the upperclass signed a statement pledging not to haze did the crisis end.

After the Segregation Incident, the new superintendent, Rear Admiral Henry B. Wilson (Class of 1881), introduced a system of privileges for the upperclassmen to recognize their superior rank. It was his goal to substitute positive rewards for the negative rite of hazing, which had previously delineated the classes. Hazing never completely disappeared. Its intensity fluctuated with the changing times and the makeup of the classes. In the 1950s, a plebe indoctrination system was introduced to define the goals and limits of upperclass plebe training. The system continues to evolve, emphasizing the importance of both the dignity of the plebes and reflecting the senior-subordinate relationship within the fleet.

Plebes march everywhere. With rifles as their constant companions, they begin to wonder whether they have joined the Army or the Navy.

Plebes learn that surviving the rigors of the year often depends on teamwork. Whether helping with studies, removing an "Irish Pennant" (a loose thread left adrift), or putting a last-minute shine on a belt buckle, plebes look out for one another. Once, during a come-around, a plebe was ordered to do a complete uniform change and report back to his upperclassman in two minutes. He dashed into his room, where his roommates mobilized reinforcements. One classmate put on his shirt and buttoned it; one gave him a tuck; one put newspaper on the floor and shined his shoes; another fixed his cover—and he made it back in time.

Plebes must learn to make the most of every minute. With so much expected of them, they work quickly. They learn to set priorities and allocate time effectively. It is not enough just to keep up. They must anticipate the spur-of-the-moment demands by upperclassmen. Some plebes use the weekends to work ahead in their studies so that when the inevitable request for a pro report comes, they can respond without damaging their academic standing. One plebe told of going to noon meal knowing all her rates and thinking she was totally up to date, only to be assigned a five-minute presentation with visuals due the next day. Suddenly she was behind, and although plebes are always told that academics come first, she, like many others, found it difficult to ignore the immediacy of an obligation to a superior. Since professors, unlike the upperclassmen, do not live in the room next door, their assignments may be easier to put off, but if plebes are to succeed at the Academy, they must learn to balance conflicting claims.

Plebes say that the most important element in surviving the year is a positive attitude. When being yelled at by an upperclassman, they learn to block out the abusive tone and the verbal insults while listening carefully to the underlying lesson. They learn to take corrections very seriously but not personally and to project an air of confidence. They realize that not even plebe year lasts forever and that each day they move closer to their youngster stripe.

Nevertheless, because the pace is unrelenting, all plebes are overwhelmed at times. Over the years, the Academy has recognized their need to let off steam. Athletics offer a physical outlet, and plebes look forward to competing at either the intercollegiate or intramural level. The excitement of fall football games and pep rallies provides a welcome release from the day-to-day tension of midshipman life. On Hundredth Night, exactly one hundred days before graduation, plebes and firsties change places, and plebes celebrate being "first class and kings of Bancroft for one glorious evening."

Other activities are less sanctioned. Before the big games, plebes hold spontaneous pep rallies where they run through Bancroft Hall spraying upperclassmen with shaving cream and gather in Tecumseh Court to chant and sing. There are also midnight "recons" to put up sheet posters, paint spirit signs, and capture souvenirs for the upperclassmen. And in spite of the fact that plebes are on the wrong end of most rates, they find ways to turn the tables on the upperclassmen. In one squad, several plebes made it a habit to report early to morning come-arounds, thus depriving the upperclassmen of precious sleep. A more traditional form of retribution was to throw upperclassmen into the showers. Sometimes it was to "celebrate" a birthday, sometimes to retaliate against a particularly unpleasant upperclassman; during June Week, it became the send-off for firsties the night before graduation.

In fact, graduation is anticipated as eagerly by plebes as it is by the first classmen who are about to enter the fleet. Climbing Herndon Monument during Commissioning Week signifies the end to what many plebes consider the longest eleven months of their lives. The demanding program has challenged them to develop self-discipline, perseverance, and concentration. They have learned to make split-second decisions and to take responsibility for their actions. Through hardships and adversity, plebes have "discovered hidden resources of strength, courage and stamina" and know that they have truly earned the thin, diagonal stripe of a third classman.

"I like it here! I love it here! I finally found a home!"

Preparing for inspection: everything must pass muster.

Opposite: A tearful farewell.

CHAPTER FIVE

DUTY, HONOR, LOYALTY:

Life as a Midshipman

Bancroft Hall, the turn-of-the-century Beaux-Arts building that houses the entire brigade of midshipmen, is more than just a dormitory. Home to midshipmen for four years at the Naval Academy, "Mother B" provides for all their needs. Within its walls are barber, tailor, and cobbler shops, the mid store, sleeping quarters, wardrooms, galley, weight room, bowling alley, medical and dental facilities, and a post office. The commandant, who supervises mids' daily lives and all their military and professional training, has offices on the first deck of Bancroft, where he oversees the running of the brigade. Bancroft Hall is truly the heart of midshipman life.

Although it appears tranquil from the outside, Bancroft Hall teems with activity within. From reveille to taps, midshipmen are on the go. They rush from formations to meals, to classes, and to athletic and military commitments. Not a single minute goes unplanned, and they accomplish more in a day than they ever thought possible.

With not a moment to spare, midshipmen must organize their time down to the last second. To help mids set priorities, the commandant issues a set of directives indicating which activity should take precedence over another. But with so many obligations, it is not always clear which one comes first. As Lieutenant Colonel Oliver L. North (Class of 1968) said, "You could strive for perfection, but you never had enough time to achieve it."

Even the most conscientious midshipman runs into trouble from time to time. Vice Admiral William P. Mack (Class of 1937) tells of standing in formation ready to march to class when he suddenly remembered that he had forgotten to bring the paper he had written for English class. If he broke formation to retrieve the paper, he knew he would receive many demerits. On the other hand, if he went to class without this major paper, he would receive an F. Quickly weighing his alternatives, he chose to get his paper and take extra duty.

Because Bancroft Hall is considered their ship, mids observe shipboard courtesies and fulfill shipboard duties. They must wear their caps in all public areas; they salute superiors; and they wear uniforms. They also stand watch. As every officer knows, standing watch is essential to insure the security and safety of both ship and shipmates. In fact, it is said that whenever two Navy men meet, the first thing they do is set the watch.

As aboard ship, everything is kept in a state of peak operational readiness. Rooms are inspected on a regular basis and must meet very specific and very stringent requirements for cleanliness and order. Light fixtures must be cleaned inside and out. Shoes must be on a rack, arranged black to white, top to bottom, with laces stowed inside. Books must be stowed vertically, tall to

The four long years we
tarried here
We always yearned to roam,
But when the time came
to depart
It felt like leaving home.

Lucky Bag, 1922

105

short, left to right, aligned with the shelf edge. There are even rules governing the folding and placement of socks. They must be rolled and positioned so that they "smile" at the inspector, or else they will be flung from the shelf and "commit suicide." So exacting are the standards that some mids resort to the dual laundry bag tactic—one bag for clean clothes that they will wear, the other for dirty clothes. The precisely folded clothing in drawers is for show only.

When unoccupied, rooms must be left open, and therefore it is against regulations to leave valuables adrift. One plebe tells of leaving her wallet on her desk in her haste to make it to formation on time. When she returned to her room, the wallet was gone, and a message on her computer screen directed her to the room of a second classman in her company. He did not give her demerits or ask her her rates but told her she must come up with a way to earn the wallet back. After thinking for three days, knowing that he was going to go Marine Corps, she composed a new version of the "Marine Corps Hymn" just for him. Arriving at his door with all the fourth classmen in her company at 0625 the next morning, she shouted, "Sir, request permission to earn back my wallet." The plebes then sang:

No pet since Dodo the Dog has been given free rein of the Academy by the superintendent. Dodo lived in Bancroft, attended classes, ate in the mess hall, and watched noon formation every day in Tecumseh Court.

> From the halls of Mother Bancroft
> To the shores of the Chesapeake,
> He has asked us every gosh darn rate
> And told us we are weak.
> He's our favorite jar-head Second Class.
> We call him Mr. Brooks.
> You will find him always in your face.
> It's not 'cause you've got good looks.

Mr. Brooks was so pleased that he not only returned her wallet, he also ordered several repeat performances of the song.

All inspectors perform the "white glove, black sock test." Wearing white gloves, they check for dust, and with black socks, they check the showers for soap scum. Rear Admiral John Davidson (Class of 1929) tells of a duty officer, Cary W. "Red" Magruder (Class of 1908), who abhorred dust. So focused was he on discovering the least little speck that he once put a first classman on report for a tiny bit of dust on a box. The fact that the box contained five bottles of whiskey completely escaped his attention. As Davidson said, "If he had his mind on dust, it didn't make any difference what it [the dust] was on. You might have had a girl in the room. If she didn't have any dust on her, fine, it was all right."

Midshipmen's uniforms and personal appearance must also meet the highest standards. White works, service dress blues, formal dress, or working blues—there is a uniform for every occasion, and each must be impeccably clean and well-fitting with all brass brightly shined. Every morning the uniform of the day is announced, and midshipmen are expected to turn out with every detail in order. Haircuts, fingernail length, and jewelry are also regulated. For men, hair may not touch the collar or interfere with the wearing of military headgear. Except for plebes, who must have short hair, women may keep their hair long provided that it is worn up in a professional style that does not fall below the lower edge of the collar. Both men and women are allowed to wear one necklace as long as it is hidden from view. Upperclass women may wear earrings, but only simple gold studs for the day and pearls for formal occasions. Men must be clean shaven, and duty officers will give demerits if the job is poorly done. However, Rear Admiral Daniel Gallery (Class of 1921) took pride in the demerits he received for being improperly shaved: he had never had to shave before.

"Shoulders back! Suck in your gut!"
"Yes, sir! Beat Army, sir!"

Few mids relish demerits, and they develop elaborate systems to pass inspections. Over the years, they have contrived ways to warn classmates of an officer's approach. They would rap on steam coils or send messages on the buzzer using Morse code. Signal flags alerted other wings. A "door salute," banging doors to replicate a gun salute aboard ship, indicated that a duty officer was on the way. Midshipmen have also learned that if a room smells clean, inspectors are more likely to think it *is* clean. Liberal use of Pine Sol, Pledge, and ammonia make for high ratings. Since sunlight reveals every speck of lint on uniforms, mids carry rolls of tape or Post-it notes for last-minute touch-ups. And because every second counts, they have been known to put on shirts already buttoned, shove on shoes already laced, and tighten ties already knotted.

Mids know that they must look "regulation" no matter what, but they take secret delight in finding some small way to express their individuality. One always wore a Superman T-shirt hidden under his uniform; others have substituted silk boxers for their Navy-issue shorts; and, as so many have done before them, many mids still hide pictures of their sweethearts in their covers.

Although it is strictly against the rules, midshipmen have managed to keep a variety of pets. Fish, squirrels, snakes, and mice have made their home in Bancroft Hall, unbeknownst to authorities. The most famous pet of all was Dodo the Dog, who first appeared one rainy night in the 1960s. He made his way to a second classman's room, where he was dried and fed by the mids. He had come to stay, and eventually the superintendent granted him permission to settle down in Bancroft's main office, where he had his own water bowl and blanket. Dodo followed mids to classes, Chapel, and the library, and watched noon formation every day from the center of Tecumseh Court. He even dined in King Hall, each night at a different table. No pet since has ever enjoyed the same privileges at the Academy.

It is not surprising that young men and women living under strict regimentation are always searching for ways to outwit authority. A successful leader channels enthusiasm and high spirits into productive outlets. Bancroft Hall has been called a leadership laboratory because twenty-four hours a day, day in and day out, midshipmen put into practice the lessons they have learned in the classroom and from their assigned duties. As plebes, midshipmen are trained to follow orders and to work together as a team. With each year, they are given greater responsibilities, and by their first class year, they are running the brigade.

A midshipman "bones" for final exams.

The midshipman chain of command, which parallels that of the Academy's Executive Department, is headed by the brigade commander. He and his officers are responsible for overseeing the professional and academic performance of midshipmen. They have been instrumental in implementing the concept of Total Quality Leadership (TQL). Based on the management theory of Dr. W. Edwards Deming, who advised the Japanese on rebuilding their economy after World War II, Total Quality Leadership emphasizes teamwork, communication, innovation, and problem solving. Although good leaders have been practicing aspects of TQL for years, this systematic approach was adopted for the entire Academy in 1991. By leading through example and by using positive techniques to motivate subordinates, midshipman officers earn the trust and respect of the brigade. Armed with these leadership skills, midshipmen go out into the fleet better prepared to be effective junior officers.

Good leadership is always best taught by example, and midshipmen are keen observers of their superiors. By watching how their officers handle situations, midshipmen begin to discern which leadership styles will work best for them. Vice Admiral William R. Smedberg III (Class of 1926) tells of being called before Superintendent Louis M. Nulton (Class of 1889) the Monday after Thanksgiving his first class year. It seemed that Smedberg and a classmate had been seen dancing at the Chevy Chase Club in Washington, D.C., the previous Saturday night. A captain who saw them knew they were there without leave and reported the incident to the Academy. As the two midshipmen stood at attention before him, Superintendent Nulton said,

"Gentlemen, I have heard the strangest rumor. I have heard that there were two first class midshipmen in uniform dancing at the Chevy Chase Club the night before last. I just hope to God I never find out who they are. That's all gentlemen." Years later when Smedberg was superintendent, he remembered what an impression Admiral Nulton had made and used the same technique himself.

Vice Admiral Charles S. Minter, Jr. (Class of 1937), learned a valuable lesson from Commander Mahlon S. Tisdale (Class of 1912), who was executive officer of Bancroft Hall during Minter's Plebe Summer. One week, Minter miscalculated the number of clean sets of white works he would need, and he had to wash one in the shower. He was put on report for being untidy in dress and called up before Commander Tisdale. Minter fully expected to be cleared and congratulated for his ingenuity. While he was given credit for effort, he was admonished for lack of foresight and given fifteen demerits and four hours of extra duty. The exec's approach taught Minter that it was possible to enforce standards effectively without demeaning a subordinate.

"Goody, goody. Monday morning and another week to excel, Sir!"
Lucky Bag, *1953*

With so many examples of good leadership in Bancroft Hall, midshipmen are inspired to become good leaders themselves. As All-American football star Napoleon McCallum (Class of 1985) said, "The Academy makes you want to be a leader. In high school, people called me 'Nap' or 'Hey you.' Here it is 'Sir!' When people start calling you 'sir,' you learn to fit into that 'sir' image. You start thinking and acting like '*Sir.*'" That is what life in "Mother B" is all about—preparing future officers to assume the responsibilities of command—and that is what sets the Naval Academy apart from civilian universities.

Academics

For years classes began with these words: "Any questions, gentlemen? Draw slips. Man the boards." (*Lucky Bag*, 1935) Each midshipman advanced to the blackboard hoping he would be able to solve the problem that appeared on his slip and thereby demonstrate his knowledge of the previous night's lesson. The professor carefully recorded daily performance marks in his little red book, sealing the fate of many an "unsat" (academically deficient) mid. This classroom system emphasized rote learning, and midshipmen essentially taught themselves. Lectures and discussions were virtually nonexistent, and many professors barely kept one assignment ahead of their students. Mids, always searching for ways to beat the system, devised guidelines for selecting slips. The 1910 Lucky Bag's "Section Room Tactics" included:

> 1—Study thoroughly the first and last parts of the lesson.
>
> 2—Choose a slip with one smooth and one rough edge so that the question comes from either the top or bottom of the instructor's pad.
>
> 3—Select a wide slip for a discussion question or a narrow one for a sketch.
>
> 4—If all slips are of equal width, avoid the most crumpled, since the mid from the previous section most likely had a difficult time with it.

Attempts to beat the system go back to the very first class of students at the Naval School. Park Benjamin, Jr. (Class of 1867), tells the classic story of Midshipman William Nelson (Class of 1846), who managed to convince the examiners of his competency in French. In actuality he had merely memorized a series of random phrases, which he used indiscriminately to answer Professor Girault's questions:

> "Mr. Nelson, which is your native State?"
>
> "Thank you, I am very well," replied Nelson, not understanding a word of the query.
>
> Girault glared at him and tried again.
>
> "What cruise have you just finished?"
>
> "I am about twenty-four years old," rejoined Nelson with cheerful alacrity, and without the change of a muscle of his countenance.

The exam continued in a similar vein, and finally Commodore Matthew Perry, one of the examiners, arose and "formally congratulated Girault on his success in imparting the French language."

Just as Nelson's high marks did not reflect his level of proficiency in French, Admiral George Dewey's (Class of 1858) low grades were misleading. Although near the top of his class, he scored poorly in naval tactics and gunnery, the very disciplines in which he excelled later in his career. It was Dewey who planned the brilliant naval strategy in 1898 that overcame the Spanish fleet and captured Cavite in Manila Bay during the Spanish-American War.

In the early days, the curriculum was as rigidly structured as the classes. Midshipmen proceeded through the prescribed four-year program,

"Gentlemen, man the boards." In each class, midshipmen were required to demonstrate their understanding of the day's lesson at the blackboard. Above, the instructor chastises an unprepared mid before he enters an "unsat" mark in his little red book, which rests on his desk.

which allowed for no deviation, and they marched to classes by sections each day. All mids took the same courses no matter what their previous experiences or abilities, and even those who entered the Academy with college degrees had to start over again as freshmen.

Given the lockstep curriculum, a plebe could open his "Reg Book" (Regulation Book) and know precisely where he would be at two o'clock in the afternoon four years later. In 1959, the Academy instituted a policy change and began to allow midshipmen to validate courses and qualify for higher level classes. This seemingly minor change revolutionized life at the Academy. Because they were no longer on the same schedule, it was impossible for midshipmen to march together to classes, and some of the regimentation and military order disappeared.

Still, everyone left the Academy with the same degree. During the 1960s, it became evident that in order to continue to attract the most capable candidates, it was necessary to provide them with the opportunity to specialize in a number of engineering fields as well as in mathematics, the sciences, and the humanities. When Vice Admiral James F. Calvert (Class of 1943) became superintendent in 1968, he worked closely with Academic Dean Ben Drought to establish a majors program that would meet the criteria of national certification boards.

Midshipmen take a break from P–work in the model room of Isherwood Hall, 1925. Isherwood, Griffin, and Melville were torn down to make room for the new brigade activities center, Alumni Hall, which was dedicated in 1991.

Today all midshipmen take a rigorous academic program strong in science, mathematics, and engineering leading to a bachelor of science degree. They choose majors from eighteen disciplines: eight in engineering, six in mathematics, and four in social sciences. Approximately 80 percent select science and engineering. But even the humanities and social science majors are well grounded in engineering, since they, too, must take "screws," "wires," "ships," "boats," and "steam" as part of the core curriculum. This course load far exceeds that of students in civilian universities despite the fact that midshipmen have extensive professional training and mandatory athletic requirements as well. To augment classroom experiences and to involve midshipmen in the issues of the day, diplomats, military leaders, and other prominent men and women deliver Forrestal, Bancroft, and Citizenship Lectures. The purpose of the academic program is to provide midshipmen with a strong foundation on which they can build specialized competence in their future careers.

Outstanding students are eligible for honors programs and opportunities for independent study and research as Trident Scholars. Over the years more than thirty Rhodes Scholarships have been awarded to Naval Academy graduates, and midshipmen have won Fulbright and Marshall Scholar-

For decades, coal was the fuel that powered the Navy. Stoking the fires was a grimy, dirty job, but nothing compared to coaling the ship. About every ten days, battleships had to replenish their supply, and after twenty-four hours of loading coal, midshipmen could barely recognize their classmates.

Never enough time: the academic dean wants you for sixteen hours a day; the commandant wants you for sixteen hours; and the coach wants you for sixteen hours.

ships as well. Almost all graduates go on to further studies sometime in their careers, and approximately two-thirds receive master's degrees or higher.

Facilities are state of the art. In addition to propulsion and robotics laboratories, wind tunnels, and tow tanks, the Academy has a subcritical nuclear reactor. The electrical engineering labs beneath Michelson and Chauvenet halls are unusually sophisticated for an undergraduate institution. The water-based oceanographic laboratory makes possible the practical application of classroom skills and navigational training. And since 1989, each midshipman has been issued a personal computer, which ties into the Academy-wide data network.

Small classes allow the more than six hundred faculty members to dedicate time to individual midshipmen. Teaching, rather than research, is the priority. Unlike the other service academies, where the instructors are officers, the faculty at the Naval Academy is half civilian and half military. Civilian professors, most of whom have doctorates, are recognized experts in their fields and provide continuity in the academic program. The military instructors bring practical and current experience from the fleet and Marine Corps and serve as role models for future officers. Since 1964, the post of academic dean has been held by a civilian, emphasizing the Academy's commitment to excellence in education.

An entire vocabulary has developed over the years to describe academics. Exams are "rivers," "P-work" (practical work) is the bane of a midshipman's existence, and all must "bone" (study) so as not to "hit the tree" (fail an exam) and be in danger of "bilging" (flunking out), a "wooden man's" (one just scraping through) greatest fear. "Savoirs" have no need to worry since they are near the top of the class. But all realize that while academics make up 70 percent of their class standing, they also have to earn a high "grease mark" (aptitude for military service) as well.

Professional Development

Under the auspices of the Office of the Commandant and the Division of Professional Development, midshipmen receive military training and instruction. Through an integrated program of academic courses, field exercises, and summer cruises, midshipmen prepare to assume the responsibilities of command upon graduation. One-quarter of their academic program is devoted to professional studies covering such subjects as navigation, weapon systems, military justice, and seamanship. Required leadership courses stress ethical behavior and a sense of purpose to motivate subordi-

nates. During the academic year, midshipmen have twenty-six hours of infantry drill, including eight dress parades. They are instructed in sailing, ship handling, and small arms. In the summer mids go to sea with the fleet, train with the Marine Corps at Quantico, and are introduced to aviation and submarine specialties.

Professional training extends beyond course work and field experience. Since midshipmen are on active duty in the United States Navy, their lives are bound by military regulations. The four-thousand-member brigade of midshipmen is divided into regiments, battalions, and companies. They wear uniforms, stand watch, and are subject to the brigade chain of command. Whereas they march into noon meal and march on the parade ground, in the tradition of sailors, they grumble that infantry is the duty of soldiers, not men of the sea. As the old saying goes, "A messmate before a shipmate, a shipmate before a stranger, a stranger before a dog, but a dog before a 'sojer.'" Because naval officers had to lead landing parties ashore, close-order drill became part of the curriculum in 1848 and has continued to the present, training midshipmen in precision, discipline, and bearing.

White glove, black sock—everything must be shipshape.

It is in the summer that midshipmen put their classroom training into practice. Third classmen spend four weeks on either a yard patrol craft (YP) or a forty-four-foot sloop and an additional four weeks in leadership training with the Marine Corps at Quantico. Second classmen take on the duties of enlisted personnel in the fleet or serve on Plebe Detail. First classmen have eight weeks of warfare specialty training in preparation for selecting their service community.

Throughout the history of the Academy, summer cruises have been, and continue to be, an important part of a midshipman's education. The first, a six-week cruise on the sloop of war *Preble* in 1851, was considered a success and set the precedent for this practical seamanship training. Early cruises were difficult. Midshipmen worked long hours at tough physical tasks, and the poor rations hardly sustained them. So hungry were they that some of them, when in port, sold their clothes and sextants for food. Except for the summer of 1861, cruises continued during the Civil War while the Academy was at Newport. Because it was wartime, midshipmen were sent out to aid in the defense of the coast against Southern privateers. After the war, the Navy began the transformation from sail- to steam-powered vessels, and the Academy's practice ships could no longer offer the training midshipmen needed for the fleet. By 1912, all mids were assigned to ships of the Atlantic Fleet for their summer cruises.

Days aboard ship provided midshipmen with some of their most

Summer cruise: "Join the Navy and see the world."

long-lasting memories. No one ever forgot the cold saltwater showers, the trick of sleeping in hammocks at sea, or the difficulty of living out of a sea bag where the article needed always seemed to be at the bottom. Nothing ever tasted like that strong cup of jamoke, java, or joe first thing in the morning or during a midnight watch in the engine room. And then there was holystoning the deck. With trousers rolled up and feet bare, the mids scrubbed stains from the teak with bricks and sandstone.

The most dreaded duty of all was coaling the ship. Whole days were set aside to replenish the supply of coal, and powdery black dust covered the men from head to toe until they became indistinguishable from one another. It got into their lungs, crept under their eyelids, and seeped into every pore. It seemed they were hardly done when it was time to coal again. "The boat has a bituminous tapeworm. Its weakness for coal is appalling. Took on the contents of another Allegheny mountain range today," claimed the *Lucky Bag* of 1918.

Far and away, the days spent in port afforded the best memories. Casablanca and Tangiers, Christiana and Oslo, Guantánamo and Cristobal—it was truly "join the Navy and see the world." On entering many of the European ports, the officers customarily entertained local dignitaries aboard the flagship. These ceremonies involved decorating the quarterdeck with colorful signal flags, bunting, and greenery, and serving refreshments on the half deck. In turn, midshipmen were welcomed into the local society and feted wherever they went. Shortly after World War II, Lady Astor invited midshipmen on cruise in England to a party also attended by the daughters of dukes, earls, and other members of the nobility. Vice Admiral William R. Smedberg III (Class of 1926), the officer in charge of the mids, tells of bringing refreshments since England was still rationing food. The young ladies gave the midshipmen their full attention until the hams and turkeys appeared on the table, at which point they abandoned their dancing partners. It was a feast the like of which the girls had not seen for years, and they found the food far more interesting than the mids.

On liberty in port, midshipmen had the opportunity to visit the countryside and see the local sights. Rear Admiral Francis D. Foley (Class of 1932) docked in Naples on his "youngster cruise" and traveled with two hundred shipmates to see the Sistine Chapel in Rome. There, Pope Pius XI spoke to the group in Italian. The mids, not knowing quite how to respond, stood in awkward silence until one finally suggested a "4N" cheer. They all enthusiastically joined in, finishing the cheer with "Pope Pius XI! Pope Pius XI! Pope Pius XI!" The Pope seemed greatly pleased.

At times, midshipmen were taken to coastal installations and defenses. On one of the earliest cruises, they visited the shipyards and fortifications of Brest, France. Because the rations on board ship were so meager, the midshipmen had permission to buy food ashore. Most returned to the ship carefully cradling *baguettes* under their arms. Later, the ship's officers found several mids clearly inebriated and realized that the *baguettes* had been hollowed out to conceal bottles of wine.

America's East Coast ports of call proved equally welcoming. In Newport, the fashionable clubs were open to the midshipmen, and in Bar Harbor, they attended society balls. In the parlors of Norfolk, many a Navy romance began. But despite all the entertainments and adventures of the summer, most midshipmen were happy to sight the Chapel dome and return home to the Academy.

Summer cruises have always been a way to introduce midshipmen to life at sea and prepare them for their future careers in the fleet. Since today they have many options for service to choose among, both in the Navy and the Marine Corps, summer training for qualified mids has been expanded to include experiences in aviation, submarines, and special warfare. Service Selection, the day mids decide which warfare community they will enter after graduation, is a major event. First classmen line up according to their order of merit—a compilation of their academic, athletic, and professional ratings—to choose surface warfare, submarines, aviation, or the Marine Corps. In 1994 an additional step was added to the process. A panel of officers interviews all candidates and places an increased emphasis on leadership for the final ranking.

One by one they enter the commandant's wing of Bancroft Hall and make their selection. If the billet is available and if they meet all qualifications, they sign up and are given an official receipt. The real excitement begins when they are welcomed by representatives of their communities in Memorial Hall or Smoke Hall and given the symbols of their new specialty. It is with pride that midshipmen receive the Marine Corps emblem, caps for submarine or surface warships, or leather jackets and sunglasses for aviation. Midshipmen consider Service Selection as important in their Academy careers as the Herndon Climb or graduation. It is the culmination of three and a half years of professional training in the classroom, in the field, and at sea, and they are confident that on commissioning they will successfully fulfill the responsibilities of junior officers.

Midshipmen hurry to class down Stribling Walk. With the elimination of the lockstep curriculum, mids no longer march to class by section.

Noon formation in Tecumseh Court: midshipmen march to King Hall as the Drum and Bugle Corps plays "Anchor's Aweigh."

Honor Concept

"Six days shalt thou labor,
And do all thou art able,
And on the seventh—
Holystone the decks and scrape the cable."
Journal of Captain Wilfred Holmes
(Class of 1922)

The Honor Concept plays a major role in the midshipman's professional development. "Midshipmen are persons of integrity; they do not lie, cheat, or steal." These few words summarize the minimum standards by which midshipmen must live while at the Academy and by which they will conduct their lives as officers in the Navy and Marine Corps. The concept itself is general, providing guidelines for ethical conduct rather than detailed directives for action in specific situations. The goal is to instill in each midshipman an infallible sense of personal integrity and honor and to lay the foundation for future ethical development. For midshipmen, honor lies at the core of the system, and carrying out their duties honorably becomes the only acceptable course of action.

Although not formalized until 1951 under Superintendent Harry W. Hill (Class of 1911), the Honor Concept has been an integral part of Academy life from the very beginning. Admiral David Dixon Porter, who was superintendent from 1865 to 1869, made it clear to midshipmen that he viewed them as officers and gentlemen and expected them to conduct themselves as such. Admiral Porter knew a naval officer's word must be his bond. Especially in times of battle, an officer must be able to rely on the word of his fellows in making informed, strategic decisions and must hold the trust and respect of the men he commands.

Today, midshipmen are responsible for insuring the high standards of honor in the brigade and for administering the Honor Concept through the Brigade Honor Committee. The committee, composed of elected upper-class representatives from each company, educates midshipmen throughout their four years at the Academy and investigates honor offenses. It holds hearings for midshipmen accused of honor violations and forwards its recommendations to the commandant and superintendent, who, along with the Secretary of the Navy, make the final disposition in cases of separation from the Academy. So much respect is accorded the deliberations of the Honor Committee that rarely is its recommendation overturned by the authorities. The Honor Concept enables midshipmen to live and work in an atmosphere of trust. The personal integrity and loyalty to the service engendered by the Honor Concept sets Naval Academy graduates apart. As Admiral Porter summed it up, "The character that a midshipman makes at the Academy will follow him into the Navy and stick to him wherever he goes. This Academy is a school of honor as well as a school for practice and discipline."

Extracurricular activities, too, have their place in midshipman training. From the very beginning, midshipmen have pursued activities and interests outside the prescribed curriculum. Nine members of the first class to enter the Naval School organized the Spirits Club, an eating and drinking society. Led by Grand Master Edward Simpson (Class of 1846, Date of 1840), who later became a rear admiral, the club met Saturday nights at taverns in town to eat oysters and drink punch. They also staged the School's first theatrical production, *The Lady of Lyons*, in an old theater on Duke of Gloucester Street. After the run, the Annapolitans tore down the theater and replaced it with a Presbyterian church. Years later, Simpson was fond of saying that the Spirits Club was the "instrumentality for the wholesome spread of religious influence in the life of the community, and shall be commended for its contribution" (*Lucky Bag*, 1945).

Through the years, midshipmen have banded together to pursue shared interests. They have established clubs as diverse as the Mandolin Club, the Society of Naval Architects and Marine Engineers, and the Ultimate Frisbee Club. In the 1860s, each class had its Base-Ball Club, and first and second classmen could sail hull-boats with the Boat Club. Park Benjamin's *Shakings*, the first midshipman publication, appeared in the spring of 1867, and other publications have followed. By 1894, class photograph albums had developed into the *Lucky Bag*, the Academy yearbook, which marked its one hundredth anniversary in 1994. Just after the turn of the century, *Reef Points*, a handbook for plebes, was first published, and a few years later, a humor magazine known as the *Log* began its career. The Trident Literary Society produced a quarterly literary magazine from 1924 to 1975, which offered "very material proof that a midshipman is something more than a uniform and a mind full of calculus," as a writer in the *Lucky Bag* of 1941 put it.

Nine of the NA Ten jazz it up in the rotunda of Bancroft Hall, 1925.

Musical groups have been very popular as well. The Drum and Bugle Corps, which first performed at a baseball game between the Naval Academy and Saint John's College in 1914, plays at noon meal formations, parades, and football and basketball games. Several midshipmen choirs sing at church services and represent the Academy by giving concerts throughout the world. The Naval Academy Ten, particularly popular during the big band era, played at midshipman dances for years. The musical produced by the Glee Club provides a highlight of the Academy year. Given the fact that mid-

Mids and their drags out for a sail on a Sunday afternoon in 1945.

shipmen are chosen for their military and engineering capabilities rather than for their musical talent, the high caliber of Glee Club productions is surprising. Indeed, a reviewer in the Annapolis *Capital* observed, "I couldn't help wondering if repeated dress parades provided the discipline for the finely honed movements on stage."

Other extracurricular activities are organized around the professional, religious, and recreational interests of midshipmen. In recent years, mids have been devoting more and more of their time to community service projects. In the "Mids for Kids" program, a company adopts a local school, and midshipmen volunteer in the classroom several times a week. They work with individual students, often serving as mentors and role models as well as tutors. For over twenty years, the brigade has helped run the local Special Olympics, which provides participants with a sense of great accomplishment. Midshipmen responding to requests from the community have participated in such activities as Habitat for Humanity, Greenscape, Christmas in April, and the Saturday Partnership for Excellence for disadvantaged youth. "Giving from the Heart of the Brigade" has provided Thanksgiving dinner and boxes of food for thousands of people each year, and through the Giving Tree at Christmastime, midshipmen contribute hundreds of presents for needy children. On April 23, 1991, President George Bush personally presented a Thousand Points of Light award to the midshipmen in honor of their contribution to the children of the community.

Social Life

Despite their many obligations, extracurricular activities, and service projects, midshipmen have always found time for diversions. From the earliest days at the Academy, midshipmen have enjoyed an active social life. Only three months after the Naval School's founding, the Spirits Club gave a grand ball that introduced the midshipmen into Annapolis society. Even though the Army had been at Fort Severn for years, the local belles found the midshipmen much more to their liking. The young men quickly discovered that their suits were often helped by gifts brought from foreign ports—Spanish mantillas, gloves from Paris, or necklaces from Constantinople.

Not all midshipman entertainments were decorous. Of the fifty-six men who entered the Naval School in 1845, all but seven had been to sea, some for as long as six years. Many regarded Annapolis as just another shore station where they could drink and carouse, and they resented all restrictions on their liberty. They "Frenched out," sneaking over the wall under the cover of darkness. Those who lived in the residence known as the Abbey were not the quiet, studious midshipmen the authorities thought them to be. Their residence was quiet only because the inhabitants had tunneled under the wall to go to town. The "Owls" and "Crickets," men who lived in Rowdy Row, were much bolder. They walked out the main gate, once firing a pistol to frighten away the guard. They congregated in the taverns in town, their favorite being Rosenthal's, known to them as Rosey's. Like Benny Haven's tavern near West Point, Rosey's was famous for its potent punch with which midshipmen washed down fried and roasted oysters. And like the cadets at West Point, the midshipmen wrote a song to their saloon, using the tune of the cadets' "Benny Haven's, Oh!"

> To the ladies of Annapolis, whose hearts and albums too
> Bear many fond memorials of the love of reefers true,
> Let us quaff another bumper and adjourn to "Rowdy Row,"
> But we'll meet again to-morrow night at Rosey-Gosey's, Oh!

Behavior was even more unruly under the second superintendent, Commander George P. Upshur. Midshipmen would appear for breakfast whenever it suited them, and many came in their dressing gowns. At night they would hold "reformed banquets." Covering the windows with blankets, they drank whiskey and smoked cigars, ate cheese and crackers, and sang songs far into the night. Poker games were common, and some even engaged in the illegal practice of dueling.

When Commander Cornelius K. Stribling became superintendent in 1850, discipline was somewhat restored. Stribling abhorred dancing, believing it to be the work of the devil, and not until Superintendent Louis Goldsborough took over in 1853 did balls once again become an important part of Academy social life. Goldsborough considered dancing healthy exercise and, in spite of his bulk, loved to take a turn on the dance floor. Midshipmen quickly learned to make way for him, "knowing well that their slim timbers would be shivered in a collision with his line-of-battle ship weight." Goldsborough brought in a dancing master to instruct midshipmen on Saturday afternoons. For years, dancing classes were compulsory. An 1869 report from the Physical Training Department noted that midshipmen would be released from dance lessons only when the dance master declared them proficient. Dancing was considered an essential skill for the officers and gentlemen of the fleet, as important as a knowledge of etiquette and protocol.

Prior to the Civil War, stag dances took place in the fencing hall on

"Good afternoon, Ladies and Gentlemen. Gathered before you on historic Worden Field are the 4,000 members of the Brigade of Midshipmen."

Saturday evenings, and once in a while a more formal hop was held. When the Academy returned to Annapolis from Newport after the war, balls became elaborate affairs, attended by Congressmen, cabinet ministers, and diplomats stationed in Washington. President Grant was expected for the grand ball given by the first class on January 8, 1869, and signs hung on the walls of the gymnasium welcomed him with "Grant U.S. Peace" and "The Army and the Navy Our Best Security." The walls of the ladies' dressing room proclaimed "Dios y las Señoras" and "Sans Vous Rien."

By the 1880s, there was an established social season at the Academy, with dances beginning after Thanksgiving and continuing through June. Although the balls were considered a refining influence, the Department of Discipline found it necessary to issue regulations in 1913 to govern midshipman behavior at the dances:

1. None of the modern dances will be performed under any circumstances.
2. Midshipmen must keep their left arm straight during all dances.
3. A space of three inches must be kept between the dancing couple.
4. Midshipmen must not take their partner's arm under any circumstances.
5. Midshipmen will not leave the ballroom floor until the dance has been completed and all officers and their guests have left.

More than merely entertainment for the midshipmen, hops served an educational purpose as well. As officers in the fleet, they would be attending diplomatic balls and needed to know the established social conventions. At each dance, midshipmen went through a formal receiving line and learned how to introduce their dates ("drags") to the hostess. They also filled out hop cards for their girls and made sure that their drags had partners for each dance. The cards were elaborately decorated with nautical symbols and each line showed a signal flag, indicating under which banner they would meet their next partners. Midshipmen had a great deal to remember, and since many had received no formal social training at home, they would often observe dances from the balcony of Dahlgren Hall before escorting young ladies themselves. Ellsworth Davis (Class of 1913) wrote to his mother, "Went to the hop and looked on from the topside. . . . I'm dragging myself next time so was getting a few pointers on the manner of conducting myself."

Traditionally, balls ended with eight bells and the playing of "The

Star-Spangled Banner," although some holidays brought even more ritual. At the New Year's Ball of 1910, the lights were dimmed just before midnight, and a bugler played taps. The most popular girl of the season struck eight bells, and the bugler then played reveille to greet the New Year.

However much they enjoyed the dance, midshipmen always waited anxiously for it to conclude, since they were allotted only a limited time to walk their drags back to their lodgings. The girls stayed either in private homes, known as drag houses, or at the elegant hotel Carvel Hall. It was to a midshipman's advantage to find his date a room as close to the Academy as possible, because it allowed them more time alone. In fact, mids often carried out a prior reconnaissance so they would be able to stay with their drags until the last possible second. A "Flying Squadron" of midshipmen could be seen after each hop, rushing back to Bancroft to make muster.

Even today, when midshipmen have many activities available to them and frequent weekend liberty, balls remain an important part of Academy life. Several formal affairs held throughout the year complement the four traditional dances of Commissioning Week—the Ring Dance, the "N" Dance, the Graduation Ball, and the Farewell Ball. Planning these activities is the job of the Academy's social director. Emmy Marshall, known to all as "Mrs. M.," originated the post in 1959. Wife, mother, and grandmother of Academy graduates, she had a strong commitment to midshipmen and spent countless hours planning special events for them. She was also responsible for the classes on military etiquette and manners. After twenty-one years, "Mrs. M." handed the job over to Carol Baysinger, whose husband, Reeves Baysinger, graduated in the class of 1949. Mrs. Baysinger has continued to look out for the interests of the midshipmen and has become an important link between their families and the Academy.

The Academy's social calendar is full throughout the year, but even more so in the days immediately following graduation. Since midshipmen may not marry during their four years at the Academy, many are eager to do so as soon as the prohibition is lifted. For many years, graduates had to wait two years after commissioning before they could marry, but as a result of World War II, this ban was lifted on April 1, 1942. Today, as many as forty weddings take place in the Chapel within four or five days of graduation. Most of these are formal military weddings in which the bride and groom pass under an Arch of Swords, which symbolizes the allegiance of the saber bearers to the couple.

Juliane Gallina (Class of 1992) made history when she was appointed the first woman brigade commander.

Meeting the Challenge

With classes, professional training, athletics, and extracurricular activities, midshipmen's days seem impossibly full. Each day brings new opportunities, and midshipmen learn that with concentration, self-control, and effort, they can succeed at any task the Academy sets before them. They are taught that before they can command others, they must first command themselves, and their devotion to duty is inspired by the tradition, spirit, and honor of the brigade.

Yet they cannot succeed alone. It is only through cooperation and teamwork that they can conquer the challenges of the demanding program, and those who have spent four years together are bound by the shared rigors of Academy life. Though times have changed, the basic tenets have endured, and the character of midshipmen has remained constant. As Admiral James Holloway III (Class of 1943) observed, midshipmen today are "just as starry-eyed and just as highly motivated as we were. There's the same feeling of pride and the same dedication."

Because midshipmen are forbidden to marry during their four years at the Academy, graduation brings a flurry of weddings to the Naval Academy Chapel. Opposite, a bride and groom pass under the traditional Arch of Swords.

CHAPTER SIX

A TREASURED HERITAGE
Customs and Traditions at the Academy

Over the Naval Academy's hundred-and-fifty-year history, many customs and traditions have evolved. Although the Academy has changed with the times, underlying precepts have endured, and early graduates would feel a kinship with midshipmen of today. The Navy itself is a very traditional service, and it is only fitting that a school that prepares officers for the fleet should have great traditions of its own. Traditions exist for everything—how to dress, how to eat, even how to date. Some customs are specific to individual classes, and others cut across class lines. But all link Academy graduates together and forge the bonds that unite them wherever they are in the world.

Academic Traditions

"When the fight of slipstick, handbook, and integration sign is over, when the last math p-work and exam are thru, when the dust settles low from the last chalk fight"—then the burial of math and skinny (physics and chemistry) begins. From the early days of the Academy, it was traditional to bury textbooks on the completion of particularly onerous courses. For years, Wayland's *Moral Science* was detested by the midshipmen and buried with great ceremony. Since math and science composed the majority of course work and were especially difficult, it was with great glee that second classmen celebrated the end of these classes. Dressed in fantastic costumes, they put math and skinny on trial, filling coffins with all the books they had studied. They paraded through town and, with elaborate rites, solemnly condemned the textbooks to death. Setting them adrift in the Severn River, they consigned the books to Davy Jones's locker. Only the top math scholars felt any sadness, knowing that they, too, would soon be in the river. Following custom, those who finished the year in the first section in math were ducked in recompense for their high achievement.

As satisfying as the burial of math and skinny was for second classmen, the "no more rivers" ceremony was even more gratifying for first classmen. For them, it signaled the end of all course work. After final exams—rivers—the first classmen reversed their caps and snake-danced while chanting:

No more rivers, there's no more rivers to cross
Thank God we're out of the wilderness—
No more rivers to cross.

With elaborate rites and mock solemnity, midshipmen bury math and skinny to celebrate the completion of their detested mathematics and electrical engineering courses.

Sweating from the heat and red-faced with exertion, plebes build a human pyramid as they work to scale the Herndon Monument.

As true sailormen, midshipmen celebrate events of special significance by tossing their fellows into the water. For years, the first section in math was ducked, as were those who shot well on the rifle range, or who performed well in other pursuits.

One of the most notable of academic traditions was that of the anchor man. As the man who stood last in his class, the anchor man was given a rousing ovation from his classmates when he received his diploma at graduation. Hoisting him on their shoulders, the midshipmen in his company paraded him through the ranks as he brandished a large blue and gold cardboard anchor. It was a dubious honor but a lucrative one. Each midshipman contributed a dollar to a fund awarded to the man who graduated anchor. Although the tradition ended after 1979, midshipmen still seem to know who stands last, and they cheer loudly when that name is read at graduation. Surprising as it may seem, at least twelve anchor men have gone on to attain flag rank.

Graduating anchor required a delicate balancing act. If a mid did too well, his average would be too high; if he did too poorly, he would "bilge" (fail). A story is told of one young man who diligently pursued the anchor spot. The success of the plan rested on his final navigation exam. Realizing that he was not prepared and that he would need a delayed exam to pass, the midshipman went to sick bay. Since he had been so frequent a patient, it was necessary to simulate a dramatic illness in order to be excused from the exam. He presented himself doubled over with abdominal pain and a 104-degree temperature. The doctor would still have suspected a ruse had it not been for his highly elevated white blood cell count. All the symptoms indicated appendicitis. He was admitted to the hospital and scheduled for surgery the next day, but by that time, all his symptoms had disappeared and he was released. Only his closest friends knew the real story. To raise his temperature, the midshipman had sat on a hot radiator until he could take no more. Elevating his white blood cell count was much more difficult. With great cunning, he had donated blood twice the day before, knowing that loss of blood increases the body's production of white blood cells. In the end, he was allowed to take the delayed exam. He barely passed and graduated anchor.

At graduation ceremonies in 1969, classmates hoist the Anchor Man on their shoulders as he receives the traditional cheer for the man who ranks last in the class. Surprisingly, at least twelve Anchor Men have achieved flag rank.

Class Traditions

While all Naval Academy graduates feel a kinship with each other, the strongest bonds form between members of the same class. To midshipmen who have worked together and supported each other through the many challenges of Academy life, the milestones they celebrate together hold special significance. The most important of these is the right to wear the class ring. The Class of 1869 began the tradition, and as a token of their esteem for

Superintendent David Dixon Porter, they presented him with the first Academy ring. Over the years, it became the custom for midshipmen to receive their rings at the end of second class year as a symbol of the leadership roles they were about to assume. Each class designs its own ring. Since 1906, the rings have had the Naval Academy crest on one side and the class crest on the other. Tradition has it that the class crest is worn facing inward before graduation, a token of the bonds among classmates, and the Naval Academy crest is turned toward the heart afterward as a reminder of Academy days.

Before 1925, midshipmen were allowed to wear their rings only after they had taken their final exam in navigation at the end of their second class year. The minute the exam ended, they put on their rings and rushed to the seawall, where first classmen threw them into the water for the traditional "baptism of the rings." This custom ended abruptly in 1924 when Midshipman Leicester R. Smith drowned. In its stead, the Ring Dance was instituted, and second classmen now receive their rings during the dance, which is held during Commissioning Week. Midshipmen and their dates line up to dip the ring into a binnacle containing water from the seven seas. Since, according to custom, rings must be dipped in seawater before they can be worn, Naval Academy graduates send water from duty stations around the world to perpetuate the tradition. After this ceremony, the couple steps into a ten-foot-high gold replica of the ring. With a kiss, the date presents the ring to the midshipman. Some mids take advantage of the moment to become engaged, giving their O.A.O. (One And Only) a miniature version of the ring.

Since 1925, the Ring Dance has been the highlight of a second classman's year. Here, midshipmen and their dates await their turn to dip class rings in water from the Atlantic, Pacific, and Caribbean. Today, rings are dipped in a binnacle filled with water from the seven seas sent by Academy graduates serving throughout the world.

So meaningful are class rings that graduates have been known to leave them behind when going into battle. In the event the officers are lost at sea, the rings remain a tangible legacy for their sons and daughters, a reminder of the Academy their fathers loved so well. In World War II, Academy men who stayed behind to defend Corregidor consigned their rings to the commander of the last submarine to leave the island. He promised to deliver them to the officers' families so that these treasured symbols of loyalty and service could be passed on to future generations.

The tradition that makes the most difference in a midshipman's life is the Herndon Climb, the Plebe Recognition Ceremony. It brings to an end the chopping, squaring of corners, come-arounds, and all the restrictions of plebe year. No one knows exactly when the climb began, but midshipmen have always celebrated leaving plebe year behind. At some point, fourth classmen adopted the "no more rivers" chant, substituting the word "plebes" for "rivers." After the last parade of the year, they snake-danced down Lovers

Lane and around the Herndon Monument shouting, "T'aint no mo' plebes." Over time, it became the custom to scale the twenty-one-foot obelisk as part of their exuberant celebration.

Today the Herndon Climb marks the beginning of Commissioning Week. Plebes gather in Tecumseh Court, impatiently waiting for the signal to go. When the cannon is fired, they rush off toward Herndon, roaring down Chambers Walk. As they reach the monument, which has been smeared with two hundred pounds of lard, they hurl T-shirts, socks, and shoes at it, desperately attempting to remove some of the grease. Pushing, shoving, climbing on each other's shoulders, they strain to reach the top. Human pyramid after human pyramid collapses as plebes scramble, sometimes for hours, to get to the summit, where upperclassmen have glued a dixie cup (a plebe hat).

Not until they begin to work together as a team do they start to make progress. Sweating with exertion and red-faced from the heat, they finally hoist a classmate to the top. After triumphantly replacing the dixie cup, hated symbol of plebe year, with an upperclassman's hat, the hero of the day is carried on the shoulders of classmates to the superintendent waiting on the Chapel steps. The superintendent presents the successful midshipman with one of his shoulder boards mounted on a plaque. Tradition has it that the one who has conquered Herndon will be the class's first admiral, although the prophecy has yet to be fulfilled.

Although plebe year now ends with the Herndon Climb, for years midshipmen were not considered youngsters until they sighted the Chapel dome on their return from summer cruise. Whatever the timing, many consider the addition of the thin, diagonal stripe of a third classman the greatest promotion in the Navy. With it comes a number of new rates. Finally, midshipmen can walk—not chop—down the passageways of Bancroft, address upperclassmen by their first names, and, best of all, go to the soft drink machines whenever they wish. At one time, a shortcut called Youngster Cutoff and other paths and gates were reserved specifically for upperclassmen. Even today there are benches set aside for various classes. As midshipmen rise through the ranks, they earn more and more privileges. As the saying goes, R.H.I.P.—Rank Hath Its Privileges.

As jubilant as midshipmen are to leave plebe year behind, they are intensely proud of having survived its hardships. Every class tells the ones that follow that it had the last *real* plebe year. One plebe in 1963 was told repeatedly by upperclassmen that he and his classmates were having an easy time of it. Knowing for certain that this was not true, he complained to his

130

uncle, who had graduated in 1931. His uncle gruffly informed him that the last "real" plebe year was in 1927. As Superintendent Draper L. Kauffman (Class of 1933) told a disgruntled group that was bemoaning the lack of old-fashioned training at the Academy, "Yes, that's very true, and it's been going to hell to my own and my father's personal knowledge at least since 1904. It's been going down hill ever since."

Adding the next stripe has always been cause for celebration. At one time, second classmen celebrated the halfway mark of their Academy careers by holding an elegant class dinner in Washington, D.C., or Baltimore. They had the hotel banquet rooms decorated in the class colors, and the band played the class march as the midshipmen filed in. The evening, filled with toasts, speeches, and camaraderie, ended with the singing of the class song.

For many years it was traditional for first classmen to hold a spring dinner dance known as the class german. For months, midshipmen set aside money to pay for the expensive favors and lavish decorations of this elaborate affair. At the 1920 class german, there were arches of red roses with stems four feet long and hydrogen-filled particolored balloons covering the ceiling. Since the german was held just before graduation, it was treasured as one of the last occasions for which midshipmen would gather together as a class.

With caps and jackets reversed, fourth classmen make a wild dash from graduation ceremonies to claim Lovers Lane. "A howling, yelling throng proclaimed to the world at large, 'No More Plebes!'" Lucky Bag, *1924*

One of the more sentimental traditions was that of the class cup. At one time, when midshipmen had their own silver napkin rings that they used at each meal, some classes decided to melt them down and mold them into a loving cup at the end of their first class year. The cup was presented to the first baby boy born to a member of the class with best wishes for a long life, prosperity, and happiness. Along with this went the hope that he would follow in his father's footsteps and carry on the Naval Academy tradition.

Superstitions

Although many midshipmen would not admit it, they share a strong belief in time-honored Academy superstitions. No one walks out Bilger's Gate, an iron-grilled archway of Gate Three. At the Academy, to bilge is to fail, and according to legend, any midshipman who walks through Bilger's Gate will not graduate. In times past, when mids traveled to football games by train, they always pulled down the shades when going through Baltimore. No one knows the origin of this custom, but midshipmen believed they should not be seen as they rode through the city. Some say they wished to remain anonymous; since they were not always popular with the citizens of Balti-

131

Bill the XVII, one of a long line of Navy goats who have inspired midshipmen in athletic contests since the first Army-Navy game in 1890.

The most daring raid of all: midshipmen commandos captured all four Army mules and displayed them in Tecumseh Court before the 1991 Army-Navy game.

more, they did not want the townspeople to jinx the game. Others say that Navy lost when the shades were up and won when the shades were lowered. Still another theory suggests that Baltimore was a perilous place for uniformed men. Federal troops were attacked by the townspeople as they marched through on their way to Annapolis in 1861 during the Civil War, and the legend of danger persisted. Whatever the reason, this custom continued as long as the mids traveled to football games through Baltimore by train.

Midshipmen have many superstitions to bring them good luck. They pitch pennies at Tecumseh and rub Rickover's nose on the off chance that these acts might possibly help them. Tecumseh, a replica of the figurehead from the USS *Delaware*, is known as the God of 2.0. (Prior to 1963 he was the God of 2.5, the passing mark at the time.) On the way to final exams, many midshipmen give the Indian chief a left-handed salute and toss pennies at him. Tradition has it that a mid who hits the quiver will do well on the exam. Tecumseh also brings luck to the brigade in athletic events. Covered in vivid colors, war paint on his face, Tecumseh spurs on Navy teams as they head into battle. And as the midshipmen march by on the way to football games, they shower him with pennies to secure a Navy victory. Annapolis children are especially fond of this custom. As soon as the brigade has passed, they scramble to claim the booty.

Admiral Rickover's nose is another good-luck charm. A bronze bust of the father of the nuclear Navy stands in the foyer of Rickover Hall. Its brightly polished nose shines in stark contrast to the dull finish of the rest of the face. Since the building was erected in 1975, thousands of midshipmen have rubbed Rickover's nose in hopes of passing the difficult engineering classes held within.

For over one hundred years, midshipmen have looked to the Navy goat to bring victories on the football field. As the story goes, players on their way to the first Army-Navy game in 1890 were discussing Handsome Dan, Yale's bulldog mascot, which brought the Yale team good luck on the gridiron. Spying a goat outside a noncommissioned officer's quarters, they borrowed the animal for the afternoon. Navy won the game 24-0, and the midshipmen gave some of the credit to the goat. The first mascot on record, the goat El Cid on loan from the cruiser USS *New York*, made his appearance at the 1893 game. Although at times they were joined by cats and dogs, and once even by a carrier pigeon, goats have officially represented Navy teams since 1904. A bronze statue of Bill the Goat was erected in 1957 in honor of Navy's mascot and now stands just outside Lejeune Hall.

One of the more famous goats was Three-to-Nothing Jack Dalton, which served from 1906 to 1912. In the 1910 Army-Navy game, Midshipman John Patrick Dalton kicked a field goal for the only score of the game, and Navy beat Army 3-0. In the ensuing celebration, the goat was set loose and ran wildly through the crowd, creating havoc. After butting a policeman, he was finally tackled by several midshipmen. In 1911, Dalton again kicked a field goal for the only score of the game, and both he and the goat became known as Three-to-Nothing Jack Dalton. When the goat died, he was mounted; he now stands in the Trophy Room of Halsey Field House.

Goats are notorious for their uncertain tempers. The particularly mean-spirited 1914 mascot earned the name Satan. He was quickly replaced after only one season. Bill XI, known as Stockyard Bill, a product of the Baltimore stockyards, was another rough character. The goats' intractability has sometimes proved troublesome to their handlers but has also helped to foil several kidnapping attempts by the Army cadets. Over the years, cadets have learned that to capture the goat, they must either come prepared for battle or secure inside information. In 1953, a group invaded from the sea, chloroformed poor Bill, and transported him to West Point. In 1972, Army's homecoming queen was the daughter of a naval officer. Treacherously, she photographed the goat's pen at the dairy farm and passed on security details to the cadets. They succeeded in kidnapping Bill XVIII and holding him for forty-one days. Ads appeared in the *New York Times* and the *Washington Post* asking, "Hey Navy! Do you know where your 'Kid' Is Today? . . . The Corps Does."

Most of the time, Army has failed to circumvent the elaborate measures the midshipmen take to protect their mascot. Bill attends all home football games, making his appearance each year at the Army-Navy game with great pomp and circumstance. One time he came in an armored car; another time he emerged from a replica of Tecumseh; and once he even issued forth from a Trojan horse. But perhaps he made his most dramatic entrance in 1971. It was rumored that President Nixon and Vice President Agnew would be coming to the game. Just before opening ceremonies, a limousine with presidential flags flying and "Secret Service agents" in attendance entered the stadium. The West Point cadets snapped to attention and saluted the car. When the door was opened, out popped Bill the Goat, to the resounding cheers of the brigade of midshipmen.

Tecumseh, the God of the passing mark, receives the left-handed salute of a hopeful section of a midshipmen as they march to an electrical engineering exam, 1952.

Army-Navy Traditions

Exuberant mids show their spirit in mess hall antics during Army Week.

In the history of collegiate competition, no more intense rivalry has ever existed than that between Army and Navy. Although Navy teams fight hard to win every game they play, it is the score of the Army game that makes or breaks a season. The week before the fall classic, bedlam reigns at both academies. In Annapolis, midshipmen hang brightly painted sheet posters and banners and decorate their doors with messages exhorting the team to victory. At meals, rounds of cheers reverberate from company to company, and foot-stomping, hand-clapping mids yell fight songs throughout the Hall. Plebes race through First Class Alley, trying to elude upperclassmen in hot pursuit. Tables are lifted one after another, as if a huge wave is moving through the mess. "Beat Army" is the watchword of the week—it is greeting and farewell, and for plebes it is the accepted answer to any question.

Putting their classroom training to work, midshipmen plan elaborate missions against the "enemy." West Point cadets spending the semester at the Naval Academy have had their rooms painted blue and gold, and exchange officers have found Army mules in their quarters. In 1969, midshipmen barricaded an Army officer in his house as they destroyed his prized new car. One by one they pounded the car with a sledgehammer until only twisted metal remained. The officer watched from his window in horror, but when they had completed the demolition, the mids presented him with a check for over four thousand dollars. Each midshipman had contributed a dollar apiece, which more than covered the cost of a new car for the officer.

Some pranks take midshipmen to enemy territory. When H. Ross Perot (Class of 1953) was at the Academy, he convinced Army's chaplain to leave the West Point chapel door unlocked one evening before the big game. At two o'clock in the morning, Perot led several midshipmen into the bell tower, where they rang out Navy songs for over an hour until the MPs managed to break in. They arrested the culprits from Annapolis, putting an end to the distasteful concert. Other groups have abducted the first captain of the corps of cadets and paraded him before the brigade during spirit events. Enlisting the help of Navy Air, midshipmen have dropped hundreds of blue and gold Ping-Pong balls on West Point's noon formation.

Perhaps the most daring raid of all occurred in 1991. After a year of planning, midshipmen disguised as tourists were dispatched to West Point, where they scouted out the security systems protecting the four Army mules. Just days before the game, two assault teams and a group of mule handlers infiltrated the fortress on the Hudson. Posing as feed deliverymen and MPs, the midshipmen expertly captured the mascots and spirited them quickly away from the post. The team with the mules headed north, away from Annapolis, while a diversionary team headed south, pursued by the West Point security detail. Eluding roadblocks along the way, the mule handlers successfully delivered their charges to the Naval Academy, where the mules were presented to the brigade at the traditional pregame pep rally.

The pep rally before the Army game is the biggest of the year. Complete with bonfire and fireworks, it sends the football team off to battle with the resounding support of the entire Naval Academy. Throughout the world, Navy and Marine Corps officers add their support. Submarines prowl the seas with "Beat Army" painted on their hulls; aircraft carriers fly signal flags with the same fighting message; and Marine Corps units take up the battle cry as well.

Since the early 1980s the honor of running the game ball from Tecumseh Court to the stadium in Philadelphia has fallen to 13th Company. The first runner catches the toss from the superintendent and begins the relay. Pairs of midshipmen run around the clock, stopping only to hand the ball off to the next pair of runners. At the stadium, 13th Company's first classmen run a victory lap around the field and then hand off the football to the team captains. Just before the game is the traditional march-on of the brigade of midshipmen and the corps of cadets. The "prisoner" exchange follows: midshipmen spending the semester at West Point are traded for the cadets at Annapolis so that all can join their classmates and cheer for their own team.

The Supe and the football coach light the traditional Army Week bonfire as Bill the Goat leads the brigade in cheers.

Throughout the game, action on the field and in the stands continues unabated. No matter what the score, there is no letup and each play is followed intensely until the clock runs down. Much is riding on the outcome. Plebes know that if their team is victorious they will be granted carry-on until Christmas. Midshipmen, naval officers, and even the superintendent have bets with their West Point counterparts. Sweatshirts, T-shirts, and hats are often at stake, but the most sought-after prize is the opponent's bathrobe. To wear a USMA b-robe at the Naval Academy is to sport the greatest trophy of them all.

Other traditions have grown up around the Army-Navy game as well. "Anchor's Aweigh" was first sung at the 1906 game. Composed by bandmaster Charles Zimmerman as the march for the Class of 1907, it was so compelling that Midshipman Alfred H. Miles (Class of 1907) wrote lyrics for it, and it became the Academy's official fight song. The gold "N" awarded for athletic achievement was initially presented in 1890 to recognize outstanding performance in the first Army-Navy game. Today, letter sweaters carry the "N," along with a star for each victory over Army. It is a rare and singular distinction to graduate as a member of a class with four straight victories over Army. Conversely, classes that suffer four consecutive losses risk incurring "The Curse." Legend has it that they will go to war before their service commitment has been fulfilled. The last time Navy lost four in a row was 1944–47, and class members fought in the Korean War. In more recent times, the class of 1990 barely escaped The Curse. Having lost their first three Army-Navy games, the midshipmen watched the fourth game go down to the final few seconds. At the last minute, Frank Schenk (Class of 1991) kicked a field goal, and Navy came from behind to beat Army 19-17.

Within the last two decades, a new custom has evolved to honor both academies. At game's end, the brigade of midshipmen and the corps of cadets stand at attention for the playing of the alma mater of each school. Even the players on the field stand respectfully as first the defeated school's anthem, and then that of the winning school, is sung. To all in attendance, it is clear that the midshipmen and cadets share strong ties that transcend four quarters of battle on the playing field.

Nevertheless, each Navy victory over Army sets off a great celebration. Once word of the win is received in Annapolis, the Enterprise Bell in Tecumseh Court is rung twice every half hour until the team and the brigade return home. Later, in a formal ceremony, the football team captains ring out the score on the Japanese Bell, reserved exclusively for football triumphs over Army. Each member of the team then strikes the bell once. If Navy has won a majority of games against Army in the other fall sports that season, the victorious team captains, team members, and coaches ring the Enterprise Bell as well. The exhilaration of beating Army remains with midshipmen long after the ceremony ends, and for graduates those triumphs compose some of their fondest memories of Academy days.

Traditional Events

Hundredth Night

Exactly one hundred nights before graduation, plebes and firsties switch places, and fourth classmen get a rare taste of the rates and privileges of upperclassmen. For a few short hours, firsties once again must square corners, chop down passageways, and address their "superiors" as sir or ma'am.

For years, Hundredth Night was celebrated with skits and songs satirizing faculty members and upperclassmen. These midwinter revels evolved into Masqueraders' performances and Glee Club musicals.

Although it is tempting for plebes to take revenge for all they have had to endure, they must keep in mind that they will revert to their lowly position at the evening's end. Nevertheless, Hundredth Night shines as a bright spot in the midst of the gray and gloom of winter, known at the Academy as the Dark Ages, and gives both plebes and firsties an intimation that the end of the year is in sight.

Christmas Traditions

Christmas has always been a special time at the Academy. In the days before midshipmen had Christmas leave, first classmen ushered in the holiday with their annual parade. Four bells into the morning watch, firsties marched through Bancroft Hall dressed as kings, queens, generals, admirals, dancing girls, clowns, and other characters. With the help of the band, they roused the other mids and made their way to the Armory. There Santa Claus made his appearance, and under the tree lay gifts for each member of the class. During the day, a service was held at the Chapel, and that evening midshipmen sat down to a formal Christmas banquet.

The Regiment celebrates as a team member strikes the Japanese Bell, reserved only for football victories over Army. This 10–0 triumph over the cadets in 1939 marked the beginning of a five-year winning streak during which Navy blanked Army in four of the games.

In later days, when midshipmen went home for Christmas, the formal banquet took place just before they left. Senators and Congressmen, along with the mayor of Annapolis, traditionally attended, and they looked forward to the annual carol singing by the midshipmen in front of Bancroft Hall. Evergreen trees decorated the Yard, and some were even hoisted on the mastheads of the *Reina Mercedes*, yard patrol boats, and the yacht *America*.

Today, midshipmen decorate their doors with wrapping paper and ribbons and string colored lights in their windows. As in the past, they are treated to a festive Christmas dinner. For years on this one night, midshipmen were even allowed to smoke in King Hall. With the proclamation "The smoking lamp is lit," midshipmen broke out huge cigars and relaxed in one another's company. Another holiday tradition is the Christmas tree in the rotunda of Bancroft Hall. Since 1991, it has been a Giving Tree, decorated with hundreds of white angels handmade by the midshipmen. Each angel holds the name of a needy child in the community. Midshipmen select an angel, bring a present for that child, and replace the angel with a red heart.

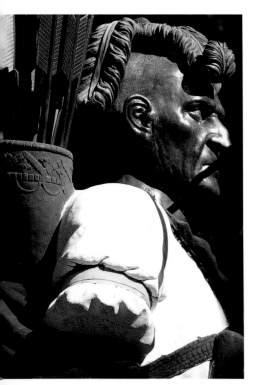

Tecumseh, the God of 2.0.

Before Christmas the tree has been transformed from white to red, a fitting symbol of the midshipmen's commitment to Annapolis and of the spirit of the Christmas season.

Halloween

Putting their creativity to work, midshipmen celebrate All Hallows' Eve as ghouls and goblins, monsters and witches. Selecting the best disguise, each battalion sends a representative to the Costume Contest held in Tecumseh Court. The commandant chooses the best and awards prizes to the winners. Inside Bancroft Hall, children from the town trick-or-treat from room to room and enjoy the frights of the haunted house built for them by the midshipmen.

Mess Nights

It is an old naval custom to hold a dining in or a dining out at which officers gather to celebrate their camaraderie and service to the nation. At the Naval Academy, these formal dinners are held by company—dining in for the company alone and dining out for guests as well. These dinners offer midshipmen both the opportunity to enjoy a respite together and to practice social skills they will need for such occasions in the fleet. Toasts and speakers enliven a dining out, while at a dining in, plebes often provide additional entertainment by satirizing the upperclassmen in the company. When the food is declared "fit for human consumption," the meal begins.

One dinner midshipmen anticipate with great pleasure is Naval Leadership Mess Night. This formal dinner, with active and retired military leaders as guests, is part of a course required for graduation and, like the P-work of old, provides midshipmen with a chance to apply the lessons of the classroom. Naval Leadership Mess Night has been a cherished tradition at the Academy for many years.

Another long-standing tradition is the annual Marine Corps Mess Night. Begun in 1928 by the Fourth Marines, mess nights have continued to the present day, with the exception of a brief period around World War II. At the Academy, USMC Mess Night officially welcomes those mids who have chosen to join the Corps. In columns of two, the guests proceed across Tecumseh Court, through the Rotunda, and into Smoke Hall, where the dinner is held. The commandant of the Marine Corps is heralded by the

USMC band, and with the "parade of beef," dining commences. Speeches and toasts to fellow Marines and fallen comrades follow dinner, and the selectees are saluted with a rousing "Semper Fi."

Marine Corps Traditions at the Academy

The partnership between the Marine Corps and the Navy dates back to the days of the Revolutionary War. Beginning in 1776, with the first Marine landing on New Providence Island in the Bahamas, they teamed up to seize enemy supplies in daring raids. In the nineteenth century, the Navy landed the "soldiers of the seas" in Tripoli, where they fought the Barbary pirates, and on both coasts of Mexico, where they were the first to claim the halls of Montezuma. By the time the Naval Academy opened its doors in 1845, the traditional cooperation between the two services had been firmly established.

In the early 1850s, Marines formed the security detail for the school ships attached to the Academy. They taught midshipmen ordnance and gunnery and later served as physical training instructors as well. Marines became an official part of the Academy on August 31, 1865, when the U.S. Naval Academy Marine Detachment was established. However, not until the Personnel Act of 1882 did Congress grant midshipmen the right by law to accept Marine Corps as well as Navy commissions upon graduation. For the next fifteen years, all the new second lieutenants entering the Corps—fifty in total—were Academy graduates. In fact, between 1914 and 1936, all five commandants of the Marine Corps were Academy men. But it was in World War II that the Navy and Marine Corps partnership proved so valuable. Fighting side by side, the two services demonstrated the effectiveness of amphibious warfare in driving the enemy from their island strongholds in the Pacific. Marines' legendary feats at Guadalcanal and Iwo Jima continue to inspire many midshipmen to choose the scarlet and gold.

Today, up to one-sixth of the graduating class may elect to serve as Marines. Because the Corps looks for a specific type of officer, it views this percentage as a ceiling rather than as a quota to be filled. Each year Marines set up a static display of weapons and aircraft and offer midshipmen the chance to learn about opportunities in the Corps. However impressive these displays, it is the Marine officers in the classroom and in Bancroft Hall who exemplify the excellence expected of those who go Corps. A colonel is always assigned as the representative of the commandant of the Marine Corps to serve as the Naval Academy's senior Marine officer and head of an academic department. In 1992 a Marine, Colonel Terrence P. Murray (Class of 1968), for the first time, was appointed Deputy Commandant of Midshipmen, an acknowledgment of the important role Marines play at the Academy.

Over the years, a number of traditions have evolved around the Marine presence in the Yard, including the annual Marine Corps Mess Night, summer training at Quantico, and the sudden appearance of shaved heads following Service Selection. And all midshipmen take pride in the Marines from Naval Station Annapolis who stand sentinel at the gates and perform such ceremonial tasks as guarding the crypt of John Paul Jones. As Colonel Michael Hagee, the Academy's senior Marine officer from 1990 to 1992, explained, it is crucial for "the [two] services to work together as a team." He noted how important it is for midshipmen to understand how the Marines think and work. Many Academy graduates will man the ships that move the Marine units and provide combat and logistical support. And in the post–Cold War era, it will become even more necessary for Marine and Navy officers to work together.

First classmen and their families gather at the Superintendent's Garden Party, a highlight of Commissioning Week.

"Dragging" Traditions

Dashing young men in uniform, afternoon sails on the bay, strolls along the tree-lined walks, dancing to the strains of a beautiful waltz—what young woman could resist a weekend at the Academy? For most of its history, the Academy was an all-male school, and women traveled from all over the country to attend the balls and hops. As one young lady wrote in a 1953 *Log Splinter*, "It is the best place I can think of to spend a weekend and I wouldn't pass up an invitation to drag a certain someone at Canoe U. for all the college weekend invitations in the world."

After the Color Parade, first classmen break rank, toss their rifles to underclassmen, and find welcome relief from the heat in the fountain spray.

Midshipmen eagerly anticipated the arrival of "femmes," especially if they had an "O.A.O." (One And Only). "Fussers" and "snakes" never lacked for "drags" (dates); they always seemed to find the belle of the ball, the "cold 4.0." "Red Mikes" avoided femmes altogether, unlike the "Carvel Hall Charlies," who scouted the young women at the hotel "tea fights" (Saturday afternoon dances). The highlight of a drag weekend was the Saturday night "hop" (dance), and just to be part of it mids would sometimes take a chance on a "blind drag" (femme of unknown rating) or join the "stag line" (the rendezvous of social pirates). Plebes who could only watch from the balcony above scanned the crowd for "queens" (beautiful girls) and "bricks" (femmes built on battle cruiser lines). As the band began to play "Sleepytime Gal," mids would reclaim their drags and dance to the final medley. As "Good-night Sweetheart" faded away, they would escort their young ladies back to the "drag houses" and make plans for Sunday afternoon in "Crabtown" (Annapolis).

Back in Bancroft, mids hit the rack little dreaming their girls were still going strong into the wee hours of the morning. Hair in curlers, cold cream on their faces, the drags gathered in living rooms to show off tokens of affection from their mids. Brass buttons from dress uniforms, gold anchors, and miniature class crests were cherished mementos. But the possession most prized was a pair of "middie pj's" stenciled with endearments and witty phrases. Before the drag mother shooed them off to bed, they had relived every moment of their glorious evening.

The Cover and the Kiss.

When the weekend was over and the girls had departed, plebes had a task to perform. They rated the dates of the upperclassmen and put them in such categories as "regal girl," "matron," "personality girl," "coquette," and "natural girl." Choosing the least attractive girl at the hop, they organized a "bricking party" for her midshipman. As they snake-danced through Bancroft they chanted, "The brick, the brick, who will get the brick?" The procession stopped at the door of many a midshipman and pretended to award him the brick. When plebes finally found their target, they placed the brick at his feet and tossed him into the shower.

With the changing times in society at large and at the Academy itself, social customs have changed as well. Today women no longer appear at the Academy only on weekends, because many are midshipmen themselves. With weekend liberty and leave, upperclassmen have many more ways to spend their leisure time. Yet some traditions endure. Many midshipmen still carry pictures of their steadies inside their hats, and they still look forward to dances and hops. And whenever their sweethearts put on their caps, midshipmen are entitled to claim the traditional kiss.

Commissioning Week Traditions

Commissioning Week is a week-long celebration recognizing the midshipmen's achievements and marking the end of the academic year. From the Herndon Climb on Friday to graduation and commissioning on Wednesday, the days are filled with parades, parties, ceremonies, and balls—a far cry from the early days, when midshipmen were awarded certificates in a simple service in the Chapel. It was not until Admiral David Dixon Porter became superintendent after the Civil War that graduation exercises became more elaborate. Distinguished guests were invited to speak, and dignitaries, including President Grant, who handed out diplomas in 1869, came up from Washington. Special entertainments were planned for the guests, and midshipmen performed military drills and displayed their nautical skills. Over the years more and more events were added, and June Week became the most festive week of the Academy year. When the academic calendar was changed in 1978, graduation exercises were moved to the last Wednesday in May, and June Week became Commissioning Week.

Today, the Dedication Parade on Friday morning officially begins Commissioning Week. First held in 1969, the parade honors faculty members who have given years of loyal service to the Academy. Later that afternoon comes the Herndon Climb, followed on Saturday by the Ring Dance. On Sunday morning, baccalaureate services are held. In days when chapel attendance was mandatory, the Sunday service before graduation was one of the last opportunities midshipmen had to worship together. For years, they traditionally sang the hymn "God Be With You 'Til We Meet Again." An emotional time for all, it brought tears to many eyes. However, as time went on, midshipmen began to exaggerate both the emotions and the tears, and the day became known as "Sob Sunday." Officers' wives who had witnessed these outpourings many times remained unmoved by the tears, but uninitiated guests often found themselves weeping uncontrollably. One year the midshipmen carried it too far. When the hymn was played, they pulled out towels in place of handkerchiefs and squeezed water-soaked sponges until water ran down the aisles. Needless to say, from that time on "God Be With You" was banished from the service, and Sob Sunday was no more.

On Sunday evening, varsity athletes escort their dates to the "N" Dance. Hosted by team captains, this dance is held at the boat house, Hubbard Hall. Because athletes miss so many social events during the year due to weekend athletic contests held away from school, the Academy holds this special dance in their honor during Commissioning Week. Two other formal balls round out the week—the Graduation Ball for first classmen and their families and the Farewell Ball for midshipmen, officers, faculty, and their guests. At one time, the Farewell Ball was the first dance plebes were allowed to attend and marked their entrance into the social circles of the Academy.

Another eagerly anticipated event is the superintendent's Garden Party. Welcoming first classmen and their families to Buchanan House, the superintendent and his wife receive their guests in the foyer of their lovely turn-of-the-century home. In the setting of the beautiful gardens in full

The Color Company Commander and his Color Girl transfer the Academy colors during the final formal dress parade of the year.

bloom, a string quartet plays soft music. For the families, the chance to meet the superintendent is a highlight of their week, and as they receive his thanks for their commitment to their midshipmen through the four demanding years, they feel truly a part of the Naval Academy family.

On the day before graduation, the Color Parade, the last formal dress parade of the year, is held. The color parade is a military tradition that dates back to medieval times. At the Academy, it was instituted in 1871 by Superintendent John L. Worden, for whom the parade field is named. Throughout the academic year, companies vie for the honor of carrying the Academy colors and representing the brigade. They compete in four areas—academic, professional, athletic, and extracurricular—and the company with the greatest number of points is designated the Color Company. At the parade, the Color Company accepts the colors that they will bear for a year.

For more than a hundred years, a young lady has been chosen Color Girl. (The one exception occurred in 1875, when Army General Edward O. C. Ord, a member of the Board of Visitors, performed the role.) Grace Worden, daughter of Superintendent Worden, was the first. The Color Girl, dressed in a long white gown and carrying a bouquet of fresh flowers, walks onto the parade ground on the arm of the superintendent. With his help, she transfers the colors from the old Color Company to the new. It is the privilege of the Color Company commander to select the Color Girl. In 1920, Color Company Commander J. W. "Pete" Rodes added a little romance to the ceremony. Dared by his classmates, he kissed the Color Girl in full view of the superintendent, regiment, and spectators—a shocking act for the time—and the kiss became part of the tradition. In 1993, Superintendent Thomas C. Lynch (Class of 1964) announced that henceforth the Color Girl would be known as the Color Honoree in anticipation of a female Color Company commander.

Often the color competition is decided only days before Commissioning Week. In 1934, Sally Mumma, a student at the University of Iowa, received last-minute notice that she had been selected as the Color Girl. She had no time to pick out a dress and barely enough time to make it to the Academy. However, her three brothers were Naval Academy men, and she knew what a great honor this was. She called on her father, a West Point graduate, who agreed to take her there even though it meant driving through the night—and going to Annapolis. When she arrived she was met by her sisters-in-law, who lived in Washington. They had rushed to the stores the day before and brought her three outfits from which to choose. Despite the frantic preparation, she appeared cool and calm at the parade.

The 1940 Color Girl, Barbara Engle, proudly transfers the colors. Times have changed, but the tradition carries on.

143

A newly commissioned ensign receives the shoulder boards, symbols of his rank, from his mother and his One And Only (O. A. O.).

Above, and opposite: Jubilation! Four long years—officers at last.

Another Color Girl, Barbara Engle, was taking exams at Sweet Briar College in 1940 when she received a telegram from Midshipman William Croft. His company had just won the competition, and he asked her to be the Color Girl. Reluctant to leave in the midst of finals, she agonized over what she should do. Her mother, however, had no doubt; she told her daughter, "You can take final exams any time but never again be the Color Girl."

Spectators find the pageantry of the Color Parade wonderful to behold, but midshipmen in their heavy navy wool jackets swelter in the hot Maryland sun. Since the 1960s, it has become traditional for the first class mids to break rank at the Chapel steps after the parade, toss their rifles to underclassmen, and race to the nearest body of water. They originally jumped into the old reflecting pool behind Mitscher Hall. Once that was filled in, they turned to the Severn River, the fountain on Radford Terrace, or even the swimming pool in Lejeune Hall. But whichever they choose, as true sailors, they find welcome relief in the cool water.

All the week's events culminate in the Graduation and Commissioning Ceremonies. The exercises have been held in the Chapel, the Yard, Dahlgren Hall, and Halsey Field House. Now held in the Navy–Marine Corps Memorial Stadium, they begin with a flyby executed by the Blue Angels, the Navy's precision flight squadron. A high-ranking dignitary—usually the President of the United States, the Vice President, the Secretary of Defense, or the Secretary of the Navy—delivers the graduation address and, along with the superintendent, hands out diplomas to each member of the graduating class. Parents and friends of each graduate are asked to stand and be recognized as their midshipman's name is called. Then those who have chosen the Marine Corps are sworn in as second lieutenants, and those who will remain in the Navy receive their commissions as ensigns. The president of the new first class calls for the traditional cheer, "For those about to leave us!" which is answered with a resounding, "Three cheers for those we leave behind!" With a final hurrah, the graduates toss their hats high in the air, a custom dating back to 1912. Before that time, graduates needed to keep their caps, since they had to serve in the fleet as midshipmen for two years. Once they were commissioned as ensigns at graduation, they no longer needed their midshipman hats, and at the 1912 exercise, they spontaneously threw them into the air. Today, children rush to gather the caps, and family and friends surround the new officers. In a final tradition of the day, mothers and sweethearts proudly pin shoulder boards, symbols of their new rank, on the graduates.

144

CHAPTER SEVEN

NAVY ATHLETICS
A Winning Tradition

The mission of the Naval Academy is to prepare midshipmen morally, mentally, and physically to serve in the fleet, and athletic competition is an essential element in their training. Hard-fought battles on the playing fields teach lessons invaluable on the fields of combat. The Academy's athletic program fosters the competitive spirit and challenges midshipmen to exceed their own expectations. As Vice Admiral William R. Smedberg III (Class of 1926) observed, midshipmen learn that even when they fall behind, they are not licked. They must call forth their best at the very time they most feel like giving up. Just as in war, holding out a little longer may lead to victory.

In addition, athletics provide an arena that develops and hones leadership qualities. Leaders must be able to assess the strengths and weaknesses of those whom they command and mold people with varied backgrounds and talents into a cohesive team. Through their own integrity and competence, leaders must earn the respect and dedication of those they may have to take into difficult and dangerous situations. Whether it is a contest against Army on the football field or a battle against an enemy on the high seas, leadership and teamwork can make the difference between victory and defeat.

All midshipmen must compete at the varsity, club, or intramural level each season. Athletics provide a physical outlet that makes it possible for midshipmen to survive the regimentation and discipline of Academy life. Most midshipmen were varsity athletes in high school and have learned to use physical exercise as an outlet for stress. Each afternoon at 1530, Dewey and Farragut Fields, Lejeune and Macdonough Halls, and the Santee Basin come alive with the shouts and cheers of players and coaches. The pent-up energy of four thousand young men and women explodes as they compete against one another and prepare for intercollegiate matches. As one mid said, it is almost impossible to make it through an Academy day without the release of physical activity.

The Naval Academy offers twenty-nine varsity, ten club, and eight intramural sports ranging from football, basketball, and baseball to boxing, sailing, and crew. As a member of the Patriot League, Navy competes against Army, Bucknell, Colgate, Fordham, Holy Cross, Lafayette, and Lehigh in a number of sports. While the public focuses on the varsity matchups, intramural games are fiercely contested as well. For midshipmen battling for company, regiment, and brigade honors, much is at stake in intramural play. The points earned for victories help determine the winner of the annual Color Company competition. More important, intramurals encourage company loyalty, spirit, and friendship between classes.

The Academy's athletic program is not an extracurricular activity. It is part of the mission of the school and as such receives a priority much different from that at a civilian school.

Jack Lengyel,
Director of Athletics, USNA

The "Admiral," David Robinson, San Antonio Spurs superstar, was graduated from the Naval Academy in 1987. Setting thirty-three school records, including career points, rebounds, and blocked shots, Robinson won every player of the year award in collegiate basketball his first class year.

Swordmaster Antoine J. Corbesier observes the form of two fencers. Corbesier, who taught at the Academy for four decades, instituted Friday afternoon contests in which the best swordsmen of the first and second classes competed in matches against each other.

After the Civil War, Superintendent David Dixon Porter introduced athletics into the Academy program. So proud was he of this crew that he challenged the world to come to Annapolis and take them on.

Today, athletics play such a key role that it is difficult to remember that they did not exist in the early days of the Academy. Except for sporadic fencing instruction and military drills, no physical education program was offered. Midshipmen spent their free time in the taverns of Annapolis and formed secret eating and drinking societies. In 1853, Superintendent Goldsborough declared town taverns off-limits but provided no recreational substitute. It was not until Rear Admiral David Dixon Porter took over after the Civil War that the importance of physical training was recognized.

Porter, just returned from duty in the war, set about reestablishing the Academy in Annapolis after its four-year exile in the safety of Newport, Rhode Island. Having observed the effects of boredom and inactivity on the morale of his men during the war, Porter quickly instituted an athletic program at the Academy. In addition to addressing complaints from alumni regarding the poor physical condition of the midshipmen, his program was designed to promote self-confidence and provide an appropriate outlet for the high spirits of the young men. Porter transformed old Fort Severn into a gymnasium, and those who excelled at gymnastics performed for their classmates, officers, and guests on Saturday evenings. Classes competed against each other in baseball, rowing, and rugby-football. Boxing classes were introduced, and Admiral Porter himself stepped into the ring with a midshipman. He encouraged weight lifting, and midshipmen hoisted heavy flour barrels and sacks of sugar to improve their upper-body strength.

At the beginning of his tenure, Porter appointed Antoine J. Corbesier as sword master. Corbesier went on to teach fencing at the Academy for four decades. Every Friday, the best swordsmen of the first and second classes competed in matches against each other, and prizes were awarded to the victors. In 1867, Matthew Strohm became the first instructor in physical training at the Academy and oversaw a four-year program of calisthenics, muscular development, and boxing. In the same year the Thanksgiving athletic festival began, at which midshipmen contended against one another in track and field, baseball, rowing, and gymnastics.

So proud was Superintendent Porter of the athletic accomplishments of his midshipmen that he invited President and Mrs. Ulysses S. Grant and the Board of Visitors to an evening of athletic entertainments. As the *New York Herald* reported,

> The exercises began immediately upon the arrival of the President. . . . on the horizontal bar and rings a number of new and curious scenes were witnessed. The bayonet exercise was a model of

This is the team that started the tradition. They traveled to West Point in November 1890 and beat Army 24–0 in the first Army-Navy football game.

expertness. The boxing was in imitation of a highly scientific prize-fight and was greatly enjoyed by the President, who laughed heartily at the grotesque attitudes and amazing dodges resorted to in order to escape "punishment." The closing scene, the trapeze act, was a masterly piece of exercise. . . . By a little past ten, the performances were over. The band struck up a waltz, which set a score of couples to whirling in the dance.

During the ten years following Porter's superintendency, baseball and rowing matches continued, but interest in athletics generally declined. The year 1879, however, saw the beginnings of football at the Academy—the sport that would forever change the tenor of the Navy program. Midshipmen played their first game, a cross between rugby and soccer, against a team of college graduates formed by two Englishmen from Oxford and Cambridge. To even the odds against the other team's experienced players, W. J. Maxwell (Class of 1880) had Bellis the tailor make laced-up canvas vests for the midshipmen. As Maxwell had learned while working with sails at sea, canvas becomes very slippery when wet, and he reasoned that the canvas vests would help the midshipmen elude the grasp of their opponents. Navy held the All-College team to a scoreless tie.

In a forerunner to today's PEP, plebes in 1893 perform setting-up exercises on the banks of the Severn.

By 1882, American football had made its way to the Academy, and Vaulx Carter (Class of 1884) organized a Thanksgiving Day game against the Clifton Club, made up of men from Johns Hopkins. A snowfall the night before almost canceled the game, but the entire regiment turned out in the morning to shovel the snow from the field. The 8-0 victory (Navy scored two touchdowns, worth four points apiece at that time) marked the beginning of Navy's long winning tradition. Exhilarated by the game, the regiment founded an athletic association with dues of fifty cents to pay for football expenses. Even officers passed the hat to help defray the costs, and football was established as an integral part of Academy life.

Even so, midshipmen hardly realized what a profound impact a letter to the West Point cadets in 1890 would have on the Academy and the nation. The midshipmen formally challenged the cadets to play them in football. Traveling to the Military Academy on the Hudson, Navy soundly defeated the West Point team 24-0. On that November day began a tradition that has become one of the greatest collegiate rivalries of all time.

Building on the enthusiasm engendered by the first Army-Navy game, an association to encourage and support athletics at the Academy was formed on December 5, 1891. This organization, today known as the Naval

Academy Athletic Association (NAAA), provides funding and equipment, hires coaches, and supervises Academy playing fields. As a nonprofit organization, it can accept outside donations, and its president is the Naval Academy's athletic director.

A founding member of the Athletic Association, "Colonel" Robert Means Thompson (Class of 1868) had been strongly influenced by Admiral David Dixon Porter, superintendent during his years as a midshipman. One of the most dedicated supporters of Navy athletics, "Colonel" Thompson hoped it would transform Academy graduates into fighting officers as well as scholars. Through his work with the association and through the prizes and badges he offered to champion athletes, including the highly valued Thompson Trophy Cup, he insured a key role for athletics at the Academy. When he died in 1930, the old football field was renamed Thompson Field in his honor.

With the encouragement of the Athletic Association, more and more varsity sports were added to the Academy program. By 1921, midshipmen could choose among fencing, boxing, baseball, crew, football, rifle, basketball, lacrosse, tennis, wrestling, swimming, water polo, and soccer.

For many years, athletes who sustained injuries were under the kindly ministrations of Augustus "Doc" Snyder, who presided over sick bay, better known as Misery Hall. Beloved by midshipmen, who composed a cheer in his honor, "Doc" Snyder remained a well-known presence at the Academy from 1911 until his retirement in 1949. It was not unusual to hear midshipmen break into a resounding:

> Iodine, iodine, epsom salt and pills!
> We've got a doctor and we don't pay bills.
> Rah! Rah! Rah! Rah! Doc! Doc! Doc!
> *Lucky Bag*, 1935

The introduction of intercollegiate play opened up new vistas for the midshipmen. No longer were they so isolated from their peers at civilian colleges. They traveled to such schools as Harvard, Columbia, Princeton, and Notre Dame and in turn hosted visiting teams at the Academy. For years, a Reception Committee welcomed the visiting athletes and escorted them throughout their stay. It was even customary for a committee member to sit on the bench with the opponents. On New Year's Day, 1924, the Academy football team traveled all the way to California to play the University of Washington in the Rose Bowl. The game ended in a 14-14 tie, and Navy athletics received national attention. As a result, it became impossible to

Star quarterback Worth Bagley (Class of 1895) led Navy to victory over Army in 1892 and 1893. His promising naval career was cut short when he was killed in action in Cuba just three years after graduation—the only naval line officer to lose his life in the Spanish-American War.

keep the midshipmen as sequestered as they had been in the past, protected from the world outside Annapolis.

For much of this century, Navy teams ranked with the best in the country. The 1926 football team was considered the national champion; the boxing team boasted eleven undefeated seasons; Academy crews captured gold medals in the 1920 and 1952 Olympics; for six years beginning in 1943, the wrestling team won every one of its dual meets; and the lacrosse team took five straight national championships starting in 1962. Names such as Roger Staubach, Joe Bellino, Buzz Borries, Tom Hamilton, and Slade Cutter conjure up the glory days of Navy athletics. In more recent times, big-money contracts offered in professional sports have made it difficult for Navy to recruit the most sought-after athletic prospects. Because Academy graduates have long-term service obligations to fulfill, those who plan to go pro choose other schools rather than lose years of prime eligibility. The service academies still attract high-caliber athletes, but they can no longer compete effectively with colleges that offer a fast track to the professional ranks.

With the admission of women in 1976, a whole new dimension was added to Navy sports. Today women compete in basketball, crew, cross country, sailing, soccer, swimming, track, and volleyball. Indicative of the strides made in women's athletics in just a decade and a half, the program moved up from Division II to Division I in 1991, and Navy teams now play some of the best in the country. On an individual basis, Academy women have also made their mark. Nearly fifty have been chosen as First-Team All-Americans, earning honors in swimming, track and field, indoor track, gymnastics, cross country, and sailing.

Each year at an awards ceremony during Commissioning Week, the Academy recognizes individual excellence in athletics. The highest honor is the Thompson Trophy Cup, which goes to the midshipman "who has done the most during the current year for the promotion of athletics at the Naval Academy." The Naval Academy Athletic Association Sword and the Vice Admiral William P. Lawrence Sword go respectively to the male and female midshipmen "of the graduating class considered by the Athletic Council to have personally excelled during his [her] years of varsity competition." The Coaches-Calvert Awards are given to the male and female varsity lettermen of the graduating class "determined by the coaches as outstanding in leadership, loyalty and consistent effort in every field, including the academic program."

It would be hard to imagine the Academy today without its dynamic athletic program. For midshipmen, sports offer opportunities to grow in

Early football was a brutally rugged contest in which the ball carrier had to be thrown down and pinned to the ground before play was ruled dead. Joseph Reeves, shown here surrounded by his 1894 teammates, had an Annapolis shoemaker piece together a padded leather version of the stocking cap—the first football helmet ever worn.

strength, skill, and endurance and a chance to meet the challenge of highly competitive foes. As one midshipman said, "Most of all [athletics] has given me confidence. Things I wasn't sure I could do before, now I *know* I can." And with the brigade strongly supporting Navy teams, athletics becomes the rallying point that inspires midshipmen of all classes to work together with unity and singleness of purpose.

Army-Navy Game

Of all Academy sporting events, it is the Army-Navy football game that symbolizes Academy athletics to the nation. In fact tradition has it that the children of Annapolis believe that the last two words of "The Star-Spangled Banner" are "Beat Army!" Even in the sweltering heat of a Maryland summer, these two words echo throughout the Yard as each new plebe class learns that Academy life centers around the fall classic. For over one hundred years, the Army-Navy game has called forth from midshipmen the ultimate in competitive spirit and has provided a link with all those who have exhorted their team to victory. The players themselves view the game as battle. As Jonas Ingram, the director of athletics at the Academy from 1925 to 1930, charged the midshipmen before the 1930 game, "The Army-Navy game is the nearest goddam thing to actual warfare that we have in time of peace! Let's go to war!"

Winning brings unrestrained joy not only to the brigade but to Navy men and women throughout the world. From shortwave radio broadcasts to modern-day satellite transmissions, the Army-Navy game has reached millions of listeners. And since 1947, it has been televised throughout the nation. In 1992, it was transmitted to two Naval Academy graduates and one West Point graduate as they circled the earth on the space shuttle *Discovery*. The national coverage excites young men and women throughout the country as well. A number of midshipmen have reported that the Army-Navy game first awakened in them their desire to enter the Academy. So impressed were they with the intensity and dedication of the midshipmen that they wanted to become a part of the brigade.

All the hoopla surrounding today's game contrasts vividly with the first meeting of the two academy teams on a frozen field high above the Hudson in 1890. At the instigation of Cadet Dennis Mahan Michie, the midshipmen challenged West Point to a game, and each member of the corps of cadets contributed fifty-two cents to pay for Navy's $275 travel expenses. The midshipmen took the train to Garrison, New York, and were ferried across the river, where they made their way up the steep hill to the Military Academy. According to legend, as the midshipmen passed a noncommissioned officer's house, they commandeered a goat from his yard to become their mascot. They spent the night in a drafty old hotel where "the rooms were so cold that bed covers were supplemented by football uniforms and even suitcases." The team slept very little.

On the day of the game, the Navy Tars took the field on the parade ground of the Military Academy, wearing the colors of red and white. Blue and gold were not to be adopted as Navy colors until 1892, and some surmise that the team wore red in accordance with the custom of Navy crews. Even-year class teams wore blue, and odd-year wore red. Since most of the players on the football team belonged to the Class of 1891, red was their color. They lined up against the orange-and-black-clad cadets, who outweighed the Tars by an average of eleven pounds each. Nevertheless, Navy's team had the advantage of experience. Using nautical terms to signal set plays, the midshipmen moved their V-wedge formation downfield. With cries of "splice the mainbrace" and "tack ship," Navy scored two touchdowns to lead at the end of the first forty-five-minute half, 12-0. (Touchdowns were worth four points apiece; the kick after, two points; and field goals, five points.) Adding two more touchdowns in the second half, Navy won 24-0. That evening the cadets hosted a dance for their visitors. And although, as the *New York Times* colorfully proclaimed, "The young admirals [had swept] all before them, smiting the enemy hip and thigh, and forcing complete capitulation" on the field, the two teams met in harmony at the hop.

Bill the Goat meets the Army Mule at midfield in pregame ceremonies at the 1922 Army-Navy game. One of eighteen played at Franklin Field in Philadelphia, this game unfortunately did not earn a victory star for Bill's blanket.

The next year the cadets, led by team captain Dennis Michie, traveled to Annapolis and avenged their loss with a 32-16 victory over Navy and its star, quarterback Worth Bagley (Class of 1895). Both Michie and Bagley, exemplary representatives of their respective schools, were to lose their lives just a few years later in the Spanish-American War.

Navy took the third game 12-4 with the help of its first full-time head coach, Ben Crosby, who had played football at Yale. By 1893, the game had become the highlight of the season not only for midshipmen and cadets but also for military people stationed along the East Coast. Feelings ran high. Partisans on both sides goaded each other, and fights erupted in the stands. At the Army and Navy Club in New York City, a brigadier general and a rear admiral challenged each other to a duel. The duel was averted, but the Secretary of War and the Secretary of the Navy halted contests for the next five years.

In 1893 Joseph M. Reeves (Class of 1894) brought a major innovation to the game. Football was a brutally rugged contest in which the ball carrier had to be thrown down and pinned to the ground before play was ruled dead. Many times players were knocked unconscious, and teammates worked feverishly to revive them. At times, they even threw buckets of water on them, because once a player left the field, he could not reenter the game. Reeves played with reckless abandon, heedless of the consequences, and was often knocked out cold. Before the Army-Navy game of 1893, Reeves had an Annapolis shoemaker piece together a padded leather version of the stocking cap—the first football helmet ever worn.

When Army-Navy play resumed in 1899, Franklin Field in Philadelphia was chosen as a neutral site halfway between the two academies. And for the first time, all the midshipmen and cadets were allowed to attend. After six years without a game, anticipation ran high. Twenty-five thousand fans crowded into the stadium and witnessed Army's 17-5 upset victory. The brigade and corps entertained the spectators with military drills performed to music and a parade of colors.

The following year's game brought another first, when the victorious Navy team arrived back at the Annapolis train station. As soon as the players got into the waiting carriages, enthusiastic midshipmen unhitched the horses and pulled the winning team by manpower to Bancroft Hall. There, team captain Orie W. Fowler (Class of 1901) gave a speech and rang out Navy's score on the Japanese Bell, beginning a tradition that continues to the present day.

The traditional march-on—the mustering of the brigade and corps—began at the Army-Navy game in 1901. At that game, the president of the United States attended for the first time. Theodore Roosevelt, an ardent sportsman, relished the rough and tumble play. As commander in chief, he judiciously sat on the Navy side for the first half and crossed the field for the second. Army dominated the game, but when Navy tied the score at the end of the first half, TR bounded to Navy's bench to congratulate the players. Army eventually won the game 11-5.

The Army-Navy confrontation did not take place in 1909 because of a fatal injury on the playing field. In spite of rule changes designed to make the game safer, football continued to be a dangerous sport. In October of that year, Cadet Eugene Byrne was critically injured in the Army-Harvard game and died the next morning. Along with its remaining regular season games, Army canceled its meeting with Navy. Since that time, Army-Navy games have been played each year with the exceptions of 1917 and 1918 because of World War I and 1928 and 1929 because of a dispute over player eligibility.

In 1910 and 1911, two undefeated Navy teams beat Army by identical 3-0 scores. The hero of both games was John Patrick Dalton (Class of 1912), who kicked the winning field goal in each game, earning the nickname Three-to-Nothing Jack Dalton. As a star fullback on the soccer team in prep school, Dalton perfected his kicking style. It was his punting that kept Army from scoring and his rushing and passing ability that set up scoring opportunities for Navy. Along with teammates Richard E. Byrd, Jr. (Class of 1912), future Antarctic explorer, and John "Babe" Brown (Class of 1914), deputy commander of the Pacific Fleet's submarine force in World War II, he delivered two legendary victories for Navy.

But perhaps the most exciting Army-Navy game ever played was the 1926 contest in Chicago. To help dedicate Soldier Field to the memory of those who served in World War I, midshipmen and cadets traveled halfway across the country for the first game to be played away from the East Coast. On Friday, November 26, they marched to the Marshall Field Department Store for a luncheon and then formed up for a formal parade down Michigan Boulevard to the stadium. In the wind and sleet, midshipmen and cadets executed drills and maneuvers and stood in the slush while dignitaries addressed the crowd. That evening the people of Chicago hosted the young men at dinner dances, balls, and theater parties.

Running back Napoleon McCallum (Class of 1985) electrified the nation with his speed and agility. In 1985, he was ranked first by the NCAA in all-purpose running (211.8 yards per game) and held twenty-six Academy records. Drafted by the Los Angeles Raiders, he has gone on to a successful professional football career.

The game the next day surpassed in excitement all of the festivities that preceded it. More than 110,000 fans, the largest crowd ever to watch a college football game, witnessed the battle between two superb teams. Navy, with a 9-0 record, would be crowned national champions with a win. The team was coached by William "Navy Bill" Ingram (Class of 1920), holder of the Academy's all-time scoring record with 263 points. His assistant was E. E. "Rip" Miller, one of the famed Seven Mules of Notre Dame. Army constituted a formidable opponent, however, having lost only one game, 7-0, to powerful Notre Dame. It had such stars as Chris Cagle, Harry Wilson, and Gar Davidson.

Navy jumped out to an early lead with a forty-yard pass from Jim Schuber (Class of 1928) to Howard Caldwell (Class of 1927) and a two-yard run by Caldwell. Early in the second quarter, the midshipmen drove sixty-two yards for another touchdown, giving them a 14-0 margin. But Army refused to quit. With dazzling runs by "Lighthorse Harry" Wilson and "Red" Cagle, they scored once, and when a Navy receiver bobbled a punt return, Army recovered and tied the score. It stood 14-14 at halftime. The momentum had changed, and the crowd was in a frenzy. Early in the second half, Cagle and Wilson combined to score again, and Army held the lead well into the fourth quarter. Then Alan Shapley (Class of 1927) intercepted a pass in Navy territory and the team drove downfield. In a daring move, Navy called for a reverse. Halfback Howard Ransford (Class of 1928) faked right and handed off to Shapley, who darted left and scored. The spectators were delirious as Navy huddled. Team captain Frank Wickhorst (Class of 1927) moved the team away from Tom Hamilton (Class of 1927) to allow him to focus on the extra-point attempt. Hamilton scraped the mud from his shoes and calmly kicked his third extra point of the day to tie the score. With the 21-21 tie, Navy preserved its undefeated record and was hailed as national champion.

From these two outstanding teams came some of the most celebrated men ever to play football for their respective academies: seven All-Americans, eight admirals, two Marine Corps generals, two Navy captains, eleven Army generals, and twelve colonels. Alan Shapley commanded the Fourth Marine Regiment at Guadalcanal, Bougainville, Guam, and Okinawa and became the most decorated Marine Corps officer in World War II. Frank H. Wickhorst and Thomas J. Hamilton teamed up again to run the World War II Pre-Flight Training Program. And Howard Caldwell made an almost impossible landing on the USS *Saratoga* with his crippled plane to save his wounded rear gunner. Many from Army's team had distinguished records as well. For their contributions to the nation and for one of the most memorable football games of all time, these men will always be remembered.

The 1934 game was also a memorable one since it marked Navy's first victory over Army in thirteen years. It also marked halfback Fred "Buzz" Borries's (Class of 1935) last game as a midshipman. Playing in the mud of Franklin Field, Borries was able to gain sixty yards, pass for eleven, and make two touchdown-saving tackles. But only Slade D. Cutter (Class of 1935) managed to put points on the board. His field goal from the twenty-yard line gave Navy the 3-0 victory.

Unlike World War I, World War II did not bring a suspension to the Army-Navy games, although gas rationing prohibited the entire brigade and corps from making a trip to Philadelphia. Instead, the game was played in Annapolis, in 1942, and only the West Point team traveled down, leaving behind its cheering section. On President Franklin Roosevelt's orders, half the midshipmen learned Army cheers and songs and rooted for the cadets. The next year at West Point, half the corps returned the favor. In 1944, the

Navy's first Heisman Trophy winner, halfback Joe Bellino (Class of 1961), held fifteen Naval Academy football records at one time. The 1961 recipient of the Thompson Trophy Cup and the Naval Academy Athletic Association Sword, he was the first midshipman in forty-one years to win both these coveted awards in the same year.

game took place in Baltimore, and this time the three-thousand-member corps of cadets was transported on Navy ships through waters still threatened by German U-boats. In spite of the courtesy, Army trounced the midshipmen 23-7.

Even though Navy lost the 1946 game, the team almost pulled off one of the greatest comebacks in its history. Down 21-6 at the half against an Army team that was a 30-point favorite, Navy brought the score back to 21-18. With ninety seconds remaining, it had the ball on Army's three-yard line, but time ran out before it could score. The unexpected heroics of the underdog Navy team outshone even the outstanding combination of Army's famed touchdown twins, Felix "Doc" Blanchard and Glenn Davis, and earned the respect of fans throughout the country.

Two years later, Navy once again surprised an unbeaten Army team. Winless for the first time in its history, Navy met an Army team that was ranked third nationally. Just three weeks earlier, Harry S Truman had pulled off the greatest upset in American political history, and the midshipmen hoped to do the same on the gridiron. As sportswriter Jack Clary reported, "Harry Truman had beaten Tom Dewey for the Presidency in a monumental upset that year, so when the President came to the game, the Navy section held up a big sign that said: 'Gallup picks Army!' (The Gallup Poll had picked Dewey.)" Though Army dominated the field, Navy never gave up, and with fewer than five minutes to play, quarterback Reeves Baysinger (Class of 1949) plunged over the goal line. The extra point was good, and Navy stunned Army with a 21-21 tie.

It took another two years, but in 1950 Navy finally achieved the miracle it had been seeking. Once again, Army was one of the highest ranked teams nationally and again came to the game undefeated. Much to everyone's astonishment, the midshipmen scored twice in the second quarter and held a desperate Army team to just a safety in the second half for a 14-2 win. Congratulatory telegrams from the fleet poured in from around the world. And the team returned to Annapolis to be greeted by ten thousand cheering fans as the Academy celebrated its spectacular upset.

Navy's teams improved markedly in the late 1950s and early 1960s. Its two Heisman Trophy winners, Joe Bellino (Class of 1961) and Roger Staubach (Class of 1965), sparked their teams to five consecutive victories in the fall classic. The 1963 game was almost canceled after President John Fitzgerald Kennedy's assassination in Dallas. Postponed for a week in his memory, it was played on December 7 at the insistence of the Kennedy family. Reminiscent of the great 1946 contest, the game was one for the record

Navy's second Heisman Trophy winner and only the fourth junior in the country ever to win the award, Roger Staubach (Class of 1965) continued to bring glory to Naval Academy athletics long after his graduation. After fulfilling his four-year service commitment, including a year in Vietnam, Staubach quarterbacked the Dallas Cowboys to four Super Bowls.

books. With nationally ranked Navy ahead by six points and only seconds to play, Army began a final drive to the goal line. The Black Knights made it to the two-yard line but failed to get off their last play as time ran out. Although Army claimed that crowd noise prevented it from snapping the ball, the final score stood at Navy 21, Army 15.

For the next two decades the two teams divided the wins almost evenly, although Navy dominated the series in the 1970s, winning seven out of ten. The 1989 game came down to a fabulous finish. Heavily favored Army led 17-16 late in the fourth quarter. With only seconds to go, Frank Schenk (Class of 1991) kicked a thirty-nine-yard game-winning field goal, and Navy fans went wild.

It was Army fans who celebrated in 1990, and they had every reason to believe they would do so again in 1991. Navy had had one of its worst seasons ever and entered the big game with a record of 0-10. But Navy had a secret weapon. Two days before the game, a team of midshipmen captured the four Army mules for the first time in history. As one mid said, "We were winning this game before we got here." Before the end of the first half, it was clear that it was a Navy day. With a 24-3 victory, the midshipmen triumphed over the dispirited Black Knights of the Hudson and once again proved that the outcome of an Army-Navy game can never be predicted. What can be predicted, however, is the intensity of every game and the enthusiasm with which fans around the world follow this historic rivalry. As President John F. Kennedy said in 1961, "It is easy to pick the real winner of the Army-Navy football game: the people of the United States."

"We're number one!" Football players celebrate an exhilarating victory at Navy-Marine Corps Memorial Stadium.

Academy Sports

Although the Army-Navy game is the high point of the Academy athletic year, each sport has a history and important traditions of its own. Fencing was the first sport at the Academy, and practice in the small- and broadsword formed part of each gun crew's training from the earliest days. Though dropped from the program in 1993, through the years Academy fencing produced ten Olympians and forty-seven All-Americans. Water polo, which began in 1920, was discontinued in 1937 for lack of collegiate competition. Reinstated most recently in 1982, the Navy water polo team has consistently done well in the national rankings and holds a superb record in competition against the Army team.

The grueling sport of cross country helps midshipmen to develop endurance, mental stamina, and self-confidence. Navy teams have enjoyed a high measure of success in intercollegiate competition. Some say Navy's advantage comes from the challenging hours of practice on the Academy course, which is considered the toughest in the East. When opponents come to Annapolis to compete, many are overcome by "Big Bertha," the steep hill about three-quarters of the way to the finish line. On rainy days, runners have been known to slip near the top and slide back down to the muddy bottom. Women running cross country for Navy have started a tradition of their own. They know that if they are ahead by the time they get to Big Bertha, they will win the race. When they reach the top of the hill, they yell out "Beat Army!" and intimidate their exhausted opponents with their burst of energy.

Two popular club sports are ice hockey and rugby. Almost a thousand fans pack the Dahlgren Hall skating rink for every home hockey game and cheer the midshipmen on to victory. Interest in rugby, the English sport from which American football developed, runs so high that Navy fields more sides than any other college in the country. Field ball, an intramural sport, has special significance at the Academy. Developed in the prisoner-of-war camps in Germany during World War II, it is a combination of rugby, lacrosse, and soccer. Now played only at the Naval Academy and the New York State Penitentiary, this bruising and dangerous sport is prized by midshipmen, and graduates enjoy telling of their exploits in field ball. The wide variety of sports offered—varsity, club, and intramural—allows all midshipmen to choose those that best suit their interests and talents.

Football

Of all the sports at the Academy, football is the one that involves every midshipman. Whether as a player or as a spectator, each midshipman looks forward to football games as the highlight of autumn at the Academy. Throughout the fall season, football unites the midshipmen and calls forth the spirit of the brigade. For plebes, it offers a rare opportunity to let off steam and a chance to escape the constant scrutiny of their superiors. For upperclassmen, football brings a sense of pride and accomplishment as national attention focuses on their team. And it gives alumni an opportunity to cheer on their alma mater and relive their days at the Academy. There is even an Annapolis contingent of retired admirals—the Golden Goats—who attend every football practice and give the coaches and team the benefit of their wisdom. Beloved Rear Admiral William F. "Dolly" Fitzgerald, Jr. (Class of 1921), who died in 1991, watched the drills for almost seventy years.

Long before classes begin, players report for strenuous, two-a-day football practices. Not even the ninety-degree heat of an Annapolis August can stifle the enthusiastic spirits of the Navy players.

Tradition has it that during football games, Bill the Goat must always face Navy's offensive goal. Since goats are notoriously feisty and high-spirited, this often proves a formidable task for the midshipmen goat handlers.

All the pageantry surrounding a game adds to the excitement of the season. The pep rallies, the bonfires, the team send-offs, the music, and the cheers ignite the spirit of the midshipmen. As they march through Annapolis on their way to home games, the midshipmen toss candy to children lining the route and inspire the townspeople to share in the glory of Academy athletics.

And then there are the rivalries—Army, of course, and more recently the Air Force Academy. For years, Navy regularly came up against Princeton, Columbia, and Penn State, and each side waged a hard-fought contest for supremacy. Every year since 1927, Navy has taken on the powerhouse of Notre Dame. Although the Fighting Irish have repeatedly beaten them, the gallant midshipmen have refused to surrender. When Vice Admiral William R. Smedberg III taught at the Academy, he met the battered captain of the Navy team the Monday after the Notre Dame game. He looked at the young man's bruised and swollen face and asked if the Academy should give up Notre Dame. The midshipman replied, "Yes, sir, after we've licked them. I think we ought to keep them until we can beat them."

The roll call of Academy football greats includes two Heisman Trophy and four Maxwell Trophy winners, twenty-nine All-Americans, sixteen members of the Football Hall of Fame, and five academic All-Americans. Names such as Ron Beagle, Buzz Borries, Babe Brown, Slade Cutter, Jack Dalton, Dick Duden, Steve Eisenhauer, Napoleon McCallum, Dick Scott, Don Whitmire, and Frank Wickhorst recall the golden years of Navy football. Outstanding players who also made their mark as Navy coaches include such men as Tom Hamilton, "Navy Bill" Ingram, Swede Larson, and George Welsh. The record books record the triumphs of legendary coaches like Paul Dashiell, Eddie Erdelatz, Wayne Hardin, and Rip Miller.

Then, of course, there are the two greatest players ever to play for the blue and gold—Joe Bellino and Roger Staubach. Joseph M. Bellino (Class of 1961) entered the Academy in 1957, having chosen Navy over seventy other schools, many of which had offered him generous scholarships. Although only five foot nine, he overpowered opponents on the field. By the end of his first class year, he held fifteen all-time Academy records. He had the most total points scored, the most touchdowns scored, the most net yards gained rushing, and led all Navy players in all-purpose running. No halfback since Buzz Borries had electrified the Navy offense as Bellino did. With his strong, muscular legs that measured eighteen inches around the calf, he was impossible to tackle; according to Coach Wayne Hardin, no one ever brought him down from behind in his entire football career.

When Bellino came out for football as a plebe, no uniform pants large enough to fit his legs could be found. They solved the problem by giving him the largest pair they had, slit up the calves. In the 1959 Army game, Bellino astounded the nation by running for 113 yards on twenty-five carries, scoring three touchdowns, and intercepting a pass that led to a Navy score. But 1960 was his outstanding season. He set seven single-season records, took his team to the Orange Bowl, and won both the Thompson Trophy and the Naval Academy Athletic Association Sword, the first time in forty-one years that both these awards were given to the same person. As his crowning achievement, Joe Bellino was named winner of the Heisman Trophy, the first Naval Academy player to win college football's ultimate prize.

Amazingly, another Navy star won the Heisman Trophy just three years later. Roger T. Staubach (Class of 1965) came to the Academy in 1961 and was coached during his plebe year by former Navy All-American Dick Duden, assisted by the newly graduated Ensign Joe Bellino. Although he started the 1962 season as third-string quarterback, he took over the offense in the fourth game and never relinquished the number-one spot. In his Academy career, he gained 4,253 yards and set or shared eight all-time Academy records, including most pass completions, most touchdown passes, and most yards passing in one season. He was the first third classman ever to win the Thompson Trophy Cup and the only midshipman to win it three years in a row. In 1963, he had a spectacular year, completing 67 percent of his passes and averaging ten yards per carry. He was awarded the Heisman Trophy, only the fourth junior ever to be so honored. Defying all odds, Staubach became an outstanding professional football player after fulfilling his service commitment to the Navy. A rookie at twenty-seven, he went on to lead the Dallas Cowboys to four Super Bowls and was inducted into the Professional Football Hall of Fame.

Both Bellino and Staubach were all-around athletes, each winning a letter in baseball for three years as well as in football. But it is not only for their athletic accomplishments that they are celebrated at the Academy. As midshipmen, both earned reputations for friendliness, consideration of others, and modesty. In fact, in an unprecedented gesture, Staubach's classmates joined together to buy him a blue and gold rosary, which they presented to him on graduation. And as a token of the high esteem in which Joe Bellino and Roger Staubach were held, the brigade requested that their jerseys—numbers 27 and 12—be retired as a tribute to the two greatest Navy players of all time.

Quarterback Alton Grizzard (Class of 1992) scores against Delaware, leading Navy to a 31–27 victory on November 17, 1990.

Crew

Navy crew traces its origins back to the Boat Club of 1869, organized under Superintendent David Dixon Porter, who introduced athletics into the Academy program. So proud was he of his rowers, he challenged the world to come to Annapolis and take on the crew. Over the next few years, the sport developed at the Academy but experienced a major setback in 1877. A devastating storm whipped up the Severn and gale-force winds swept away the boat house and fifteen shells. Not until 1892 was crew revived, largely due to the efforts of Winston Churchill (Class of 1894), who later became a famous novelist.

Despite the lack of money, boats, and time for practice, Churchill managed to put together a class four, and the next year a class eight, to compete against other schools. Although many had never rowed before, Churchill's enthusiasm convinced a number of his classmates to come out for this grueling sport. He sometimes used the steak served only at the training table as an added incentive. He even persuaded the midshipmen to contribute more than eight hundred dollars toward the purchase of shells.

From the tenacity and vision of Churchill, there developed an outstanding tradition of crew at the Academy. Three times Navy has sent eight-man shells to the Olympics, bringing home gold medals from Antwerp in 1920 and from Helsinki in 1952. Famous men who lettered in crew include astronaut Rear Admiral Alan B. Shepard, Jr. (Class of 1945), and Admiral Chester W. Nimitz (Class of 1905), who pulled stroke. Today, there are lightweight and heavyweight men's squads and women's crews, all of which compete on the varsity level. This arduous sport demands total dedication and enormous physical stamina. Rowers practice six days a week, up to four hours a session. They lift weights, run, and put in their time on rowing machines. But most of all, they spend long, exhausting hours on the water slicing through the waves until they pull together as one. As the sign in Hubbard Hall admonishes, "Go hard or go home."

Those qualities so essential to success as midshipmen and as officers in the fleet are exemplified by Navy rowers—hard work, perseverance, and teamwork. Admiral Kinnaird R. McKee (Class of 1951) tells of accompanying Navy crews to New London for a race in the late 1970s when he was superintendent. At the time, Harvard dominated the sport, and although the Navy program was making great strides, Harvard was clearly expected to win it all. Both the plebes and junior varsity rowed good races but could not overcome Harvard's strength. After these crews had raced, Harvard's winning

Navy crew, which traces its origins back to the Boat Club of 1869, has an outstanding record at the Academy. Three times Navy has sent eight-man shells to the Olympics, bringing home gold medals from Antwerp in 1920 and from Helsinki in 1952.

teams headed back to the boat house for showers, but the midshipmen stayed to cheer Navy on in the next race. In a major upset, the varsity triumphed, and as the Harvard varsity eight dejectedly rowed in, their coach followed in a motorboat screaming at them over a bullhorn. The three Navy crews stood together rejoicing in the varsity's victory. Admiral McKee turned to a Harvard supporter next to him and said, "You asked about the difference between the Naval Academy and other schools. This is it."

Boxing

It's a gala crowd that makes its appearance at Macdonough Hall for the opening bout of the Academy boxing season. Gold braid and gold lace adorn the officers' full dress uniforms . . . civilian tuxes interweave the background . . . and studding the entire atmosphere are the women's multi-colored formal gowns, bespeckled here with a red rose corsage—there with a white gardenia. A rousing cheer goes up from the Navy rooting section as the blue and gold boxers trot out to their ringside seats. Trainers and managers give them a last minute pep talk . . . then the 120 pounders step between the ropes and into the ring. The loud speaking system blares forth with the two contestants' names . . . the lights go out, only the giant ring lights glare down on the boxers in their corners . . . "silence" flashes . . . the crowd hushes in watchful expectation . . . there goes the bell—and the start of another boxing season at Annapolis!

Lucky Bag, 1941

Boxing, a two-year requirement for all male midshipmen, fosters self-confidence and poise under pressure. The midwinter Brigade Boxing Championships, in which regimental winners vie for victory, light up the "Dark Ages" at the Academy.

For years, boxing matches were formal affairs, usually held on Saturday evenings before Academy hops. Silence reigned during the bout, with cheering allowed only between rounds. The elegantly attired fans and the hushed atmosphere elevated Academy boxing high above the sordid milieu of the professional ring. Midshipmen escorted their young ladies, who wore evening gowns and carried their dancing slippers ready for the ball to follow. This period was the heyday of Academy boxing, during which Navy remained undefeated for eleven straight years and won six national titles.

Begun under Superintendent Porter in 1865 as a recreational activity, boxing became a varsity sport in 1920. As time went on, many large universities started to recruit experienced boxers who had come from the Golden Gloves program or the enlisted ranks of the military. With true amateurs mismatched against semipros, the sport became dangerous. As a result, the Academy made boxing a club sport, which nevertheless continued to enjoy great popularity. Even today, all male plebes and third classmen are required to box. The sport develops agility, resourcefulness, and stamina. It instills self-confidence and teaches midshipmen to respond coolly under pressure.

Once boxing became a club sport, battalion boxers began to battle each other for Academy championships. At the finals, still major events, the brigade cheers on the contenders. One famous match in 1967 pitted two future Marines against each other—Oliver North, later assistant to President Reagan's national security advisor, and James Webb, a Vietnam hero who would become Secretary of the Navy. Webb was favored since he had had previous experience, but North fought aggressively and managed to win the decision. Both North and Webb boxed under Emerson Smith, one of the three legendary Navy coaches.

The first of the three eminent coaches, Hamilton Murrell "Spike" Webb, came to the Academy in 1919 after serving as the boxing coach of the American Expeditionary Force for the Inter-Allied games in Paris. To win the job, the five-foot-four, 131-pound Webb had to climb into the ring with boxing instructor Joe Stanton, who was six feet tall and weighed 190 pounds. Webb easily disposed of Stanton, then turned to face Frank Sazama, the USNA coach, who was built along Stanton's lines. After two rounds, Webb proved he was the man for the job, and he was hired on the spot.

Hal Zabrowski (Class of 1992) heads the ball in a hard-fought soccer match against George Mason University.

Under Webb, the "man who taught the Navy to fight," Navy teams dominated college boxing, with such fighters as Harry Henderson, Duke Crinkley, Richie Collins, Moon Chapple, and Mike Wallace. The best fighter Webb ever coached, and, many feel, the best ever to come out of the Naval Academy, was Slade Cutter (Class of 1935), who won eighteen straight bouts for the team. According to Webb, Cutter did everything right. On graduation, Cutter was offered fifty thousand dollars to turn professional. Webb believed he was easily on a par with heavyweight champions Primo Carnera and Max Baer. Fortunately for the Navy, Cutter turned down the offer, and during World War II, he became one of the most decorated submariners in the fleet.

In fact, fifty-three of Webb's fighters won medals for courageous service. As Vice Admiral Robert B. Pirie (Class of 1926) said, "In my opinion Spike had as much to do with winning World War II as any man in uniform. He taught guts to midshipmen. The things we learned from him enabled us to stick it out when the going got rough." Webb retired in 1954 after thirty-five years at the Academy, six national championships, and eleven straight undefeated seasons. At a testimonial dinner held for him in 1961, he was honored for his Navy days as well as for his record as the coach of four Olympic teams and of such famous boxers as Gene Tunney, Eddie Eagan, and Sugar Ray Robinson.

Tony Rubino joined the Academy staff in 1948 as Spike Webb's assistant, and he was later named deputy director of the Physical Education Department. A great athlete, he was runner-up at 145 pounds in the intercollegiate championships in his college days. During World War II, Rubino was selected to instruct Navy pilots in physical training at the Academy and soon after the war went back to Annapolis as a lieutenant commander to work with Webb. Taking over as head coach in 1954, he continued to stress the value of boxing for future naval officers, as Webb had done before him. Rubino strongly believed that "boxing most easily helps a midshipman to relax and keep calm and poised under pressure. It teaches self-confidence. The conquest of fear is the greatest conquest of all."

Emerson Smith, the third member of the boxing triumvirate, took over the program in 1965. He emphasized skill and technique instead of overpowering force. For every hour of instruction on offense, he spent six hours of instruction on defense. Safety was his overriding concern, and in addition to teaching strategy, he worked for years to develop safer protective equipment. With a mechanical engineering professor at the Academy, he designed thumbless boxing gloves and foam-padded headgear that reduced the impact of a punch by up to 50 percent. His picture still appears on a number of Everlast boxing products. In 1980, he was appointed safety chairman for the National Collegiate Boxing Association and in 1988 was named to the same position for the United States of America Amateur Boxing Association. Midshipmen who trained under him knew his belief that those who wear the uniform must be able to defend it and well remember his three cardinal rules of the sport: "Keep your hands up, your feet moving and your ass off the deck."

Boxing remains a vivid memory for all male midshipmen. For some, it is the stench of the sweat-soaked equipment and the box of slimy, used mouthpieces. For others, it is the sinking feeling in the pit of the stomach when the bell clangs for another round. For still others, it is the pride of representing their regiment in the brigade championships. But for all, it is the accomplishment of having stood alone in the ring and having bravely met the challenge. In later years, they can draw on the strength they found in the ring and face an enemy with courage and confidence.

Wrestling

For over seventy-five years, a triad of coaches that headed the Naval Academy's wrestling program produced remarkable teams that posted more than seventy winning seasons. In 1912 John Schutz, who had organized the first varsity team in 1909, returned to the Academy and coached wrestling for the next twenty-six years. Under his direction, Navy wrestling rose to national prominence and from 1918 to 1925 achieved an extraordinary 47-3-1 record. Eight members of those teams competed in the 1920 and 1924 Olympics, including Frank Maichle (Class of 1920). Maichle had led the 1919 Navy team to an undefeated season, blanking powerful 1918 national champion Penn State.

In 1939, Ray Swartz took over as coach and two years later helped his team gain entrance to the prestigious Eastern Intercollegiate Wrestling Association (EIWA). Over the six years from 1943 to 1948, Swartz's wrestlers set a still-unbroken Academy record of forty-eight straight meet victories and won the EIWA championships four years in a row. Much to the midshipmen's delight, three of those EIWA victories were over Army. Dual meets with Army began in 1957, and Navy's success against the cadets has been legendary. The midshipmen took the first meet, and since 1962, Navy has gone undefeated against the Black Knights.

Notable wrestlers coached by Swartz included Malcolm W. "Mickey" MacDonald (Class of 1946), John O. "Bo" Coppedge (Class of 1947), and John A. Fletcher (Class of 1948). Wrestling at 121 pounds, Mickey MacDonald posted a record of 30-0-0 during his Academy career, won three EIWA championships, and was voted outstanding wrestler of America in 1944 by the National AAU. Bo Coppedge, who later became the Academy's athletic director, had an outstanding season in 1944, going 7-0 in dual meets and coming in a close second at the Eastern Championships. Johnny Fletcher, the only Navy man ever to be named EIWA's outstanding wrestler twice, died in a plane crash. He is memorialized by a trophy given annually in his name to the wrestler with the most team points in EIWA competition.

The third member of the coaching triad, Ed Peery, came to the Academy in 1961 and coached for twenty-seven years. A member of the famous Peery wrestling family, he, like his father and older brother, won three NCAA championships as an undergraduate. Starting with Peery's second season, Navy began its winning ways over Army and never lost again while he was coach. In 1968, he was named NCAA Coach of the Year and later was inducted, along with his father and brother, into the Amateur Wrestling Hall of Fame. Among the superb wrestlers he coached was Lloyd W. Keaser (Class of 1972), who won the Easterns three times and brought home the silver medal for the United States from the 1976 Olympics—the best showing of any Navy wrestler in Olympic history. When Peery retired as coach in 1987, he handed the reins to his assistant Reg Wicks and left an amazing record of 311 wins, only 90 losses, and 14 ties. Wicks has continued to enhance Navy's solid competitive wrestling program, and as his teams rack up victories, the legendary triad is on its way to becoming a quartet.

Lacrosse

Navy lacrosse owes its beginnings to two former Johns Hopkins players, Frank Breyer and Bill Hudgins. They loved the sport so much that while practicing law in Baltimore, they traveled to Annapolis three times a week in 1907 to coach the fledgling team they had helped to organize. The next year, Navy began intercollegiate play, and although it lost both of its games, the sport proved immensely popular. By 1914, it could post an undefeated season and had more wins that year than any other college team.

In fact, it is impossible to talk about Navy lacrosse without cataloguing the impressive records achieved over the years. From 1917 to 1923, Navy went undefeated and in nine games in 1920 gave up only six goals. The first official coach, George Finlayson, retired in 1935 after producing eleven unbeaten teams in twenty-five years. The eight consecutive national championships that Navy won or shared between 1960 and 1967 marked the golden age of Navy lacrosse. In that era, Navy teams coached by Willis Bilderback won five straight titles outright from 1962 to 1966, losing only one game in all those years. Overall, the Academy captured seventeen national championships and has produced more than one hundred First-Team All-Americans.

Six of Navy's national titles came under the legendary William H. "Dinty" Moore III, who coached from 1936 to 1958. His players included such greats as Robert J. Booze (Class of 1944), who scored a record 8 goals in one game, and Lee Chambers (Class of 1949), who scored an astonishing 148 goals in his four years at the Academy. Moore's own fortitude and dedication were evidenced in the 1954 season. During the game against Duke, Moore's leg was severely fractured as he stood on the sidelines. He refused medical care until the game's end. When the X-rays revealed the seriousness of the injury, he was ordered to bed for three months. Nevertheless, he insisted on coaching his team from a wheelchair as Navy beat Army for the

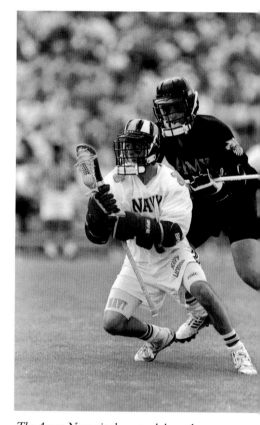

The Army-Navy rivalry extends beyond the football field. In 1924, the Navy lacrosse team defeated the Cadets 5–0 at West Point in their first match-up, and each spring, the two academies fight for dominance in this grueling sport.

national title. Moore's example inspired not only his players but future coaches as well. Both Dick Szlasa and Bryan Matthews have continued in the winning tradition, and Navy lacrosse remains one of the most respected programs in the country.

Basketball

Basketball began at the Academy in 1907, and competition with Army dates back to 1920. Particularly memorable was the 1933 Army game, when Charles E. Loughlin (Class of 1933) scored more points—twenty-five—than the entire Army team, and Navy cruised to a 51-24 victory. In another memorable game, Army set out to avenge its football loss to Navy in 1963—its fourth defeat in as many years. General William Westmoreland, superintendent of West Point, invited Army VIPs from the Pentagon to witness the win he was anticipating. But Navy coach Ben Carnevale had a very different outcome in mind. He put in his secret weapon, football great Roger Staubach, giving him the job of guarding Cadet Joe Kosciusko, who had scored thirty points in a game the week before. Staubach held him to only six points in the first half, and Kosciusko was benched for the rest of the game. A disgruntled Westmoreland confronted the Navy coach afterward and said, "Damn it, Carnevale, Staubach's no basketball player." Carnevale replied, "No, sir, but he's a winner."

Carnevale himself was a winner. In the twenty years he coached Navy basketball, his teams put together 308 victories and played in six postseason tournaments. After posting a 16-1 record in his first season, Carnevale was named Collegiate Coach of the Year, and his team received Navy's first bid ever to the NCAA Tournament. Elected to the National Basketball Hall of Fame, Ben Carnevale is the all-time winningest coach in Navy history.

Although Carnevale coached a number of outstanding players, Paul Evans and Pete Hermann were the coaches who had the opportunity to work with the greatest star ever to play basketball for Navy—David Robinson. When Robinson graduated in 1987, he held or shared thirty-three Naval Academy records, including 2,669 career points, 1,314 rebounds, and a 61.3 field goal shooting percentage. His fourteen blocked shots in the game against University of North Carolina-Wilmington on January 4, 1986, set an NCAA record, as did his 207 blocked shots for the 1985–86 season. In fact, in that year only the Louisville Cardinals, the national champions, blocked more shots as a team than Robinson did single-handedly.

There was little in Robinson's high school career to predict that he would become a superstar. He quit the team his junior year because he was not getting enough playing time, and he only played as a senior because the coach at his new high school recruited him for his height. At six-foot-five, he was just one inch shy of the maximum qualifying height for candidates at the Naval Academy. Unfortunately, he missed the first four games of his plebe season as a result of a broken hand suffered in boxing class. In his third class year, Robinson began to shine, leading the team in scoring and rebounds. By the time he graduated, he had grown to seven-foot-one and had broken almost every Academy basketball record.

In addition to his phenomenal personal statistics, he was an outstanding team player whose main concern was for Navy's success. As he said, "Good players help their team win. All the points and rebounds in the world don't matter if you lose." So popular was he throughout the country, applications to the Naval Academy increased dramatically during his years. Because of the glory he brought to Navy, Commandant Stephen Chadwick canceled afternoon events one Sunday in the summer of 1986 to permit Robinson's classmates and the new plebes to watch him play with the United States team in the World Championship game in Madrid.

Because of his height, Robinson was released from active service after two years instead of five. He joined the San Antonio Spurs of the NBA in 1989 and was named Rookie of the Year. Known to his fans as "The Admiral," he has repeatedly been selected for the All-Star Team and represented the United States as a member of the gold-medal-winning "Dream Team" in the 1992 Olympics. Over the years, he has maintained strong ties to the Naval Academy and has enhanced the prestige of the Navy's basketball program.

Along with basketball, Navy women compete in eight other varsity sports. Although women have been at the Naval Academy only since 1976, already more than fifty have been named First Team All-Americans.

Croquet

Probably the most unusual sporting event at the Academy is the annual croquet battle against neighboring Saint John's College. In 1983, the Johnnies challenged the midshipmen to meet them for a match at the four-hundred-year-old Liberty Tree, under which Annapolitan patriots had gathered in 1765 to protest the Stamp Act. Each spring midshipmen, nattily dressed in an approximation of the old Dress Baker uniforms—double-breasted navy blue jackets, white slacks, white shoes, and bow ties—face the eccentrically attired Saint John's team.

While midshipmen plan strategy and take the contest quite seriously, the Johnnies prefer to revel in the atmosphere. Young ladies in flowing gowns proffer hors d'oeuvres and champagne as classical music plays in the background. Spectators, dressed in tie-dyed clothes and sandals, shorts and T-shirts, or even formal wear, come and go throughout the match, which sometimes lasts until dusk. Cheers, many reflecting the enormous contrast between the two schools, spontaneously erupt from the crowd. While midshipmen urge their team on with the traditional "4N" cheer, Johnnies chant, "You can keep your deep blue sea, we have our philosophy." So far, Saint John's holds the edge in the series, but the midshipmen hope to have the Academy's name engraved on the Annapolis Cup as often as their opponent's. They want the winner's cup, displayed at the Little Campus Restaurant in town, to attest to another victorious Navy team.

Sailing

Perhaps no sport is more appropriate to the Academy than sailing. After all, when the Academy was founded in 1845, wooden ships plied the seas powered only by wind, and all officers had to master the art of sailing. The Midshipmen Sailing Squadron was formed in 1847, the third-oldest yacht club in the country according to *Lloyd's North American Yachting Register*. Only the Detroit Boat Club and New York Yacht Club are older. Four years later, summer practice cruises began, giving midshipmen practical experience at sea. In 1859, the USS *Constitution*, "Old Ironsides," made famous in the War of 1812, came to the Academy as a school ship. When the Civil War broke out, the midshipmen sailed her to the safety of Newport. Other famous ships, such as the *Santee*, *Reina Mercedes*, *Chesapeake*, and the well-loved yacht *America*, were employed to teach midshipmen the rudiments of sailing.

Perhaps no sport is more appropriate to the Naval Academy than sailing, and by the time they graduate, all midshipmen are competent sailors.

With the changeover from wind- to steam-powered vessels in the twentieth century, sailing took a backseat at the Academy, and the program was not revived until the 1930s. In 1936, the Midshipmen's Boat Club was reorganized. In that same year, Vadim Makaroff presented the seventy-two-foot ocean-racing yacht *Vamarie* to the Academy. The Midshipmen's Boat Club raced her on the Chesapeake Bay in 1937, and on graduation, several members of the class of 1938, including future Rear Admiral Robert W. McNitt, sailed with a Navy captain and crew in the Newport-to-Bermuda race. With their capable performance, Navy sailing once again gained the respect of the sailing world. Put on hold during the war years, the sailing program flourished once again under the leadership of Superintendent James L. Holloway, Jr. (Class of 1919), and De Coursey Fales, commodore of the New York Yacht Club. Commodore Fales founded the Fales Committee, which still advises the superintendent on all aspects of Navy sailing.

The program received several real boosts in the 1970s. First, the Naval Academy Sailing Foundation (originally called the Naval Academy Sailing Association) was formed. This private organization has the authority to accept donations of boats for the Academy. After one year, those donated boats not needed for the Academy program can be sold, with the proceeds going to strengthen the sailing program. Second, the Robert Crown Sailing Center, headquarters of Navy sailing and home of the Intercollegiate Sailing Hall of Fame, was donated by the Crown family. Third, Superintendent William P. Mack (Class of 1937) convinced the athletic director to award varsity status to the sailing team. Admiral Mack also persuaded Alex Grosvenor (Class of 1950) to head up Academy sailing. Under Grosvenor's direction, midshipmen sailors scraped, painted, and maintained Academy boats, practiced long hours in good weather and bad, and made Navy sailing the top-ranked program in the country.

Today, the program is divided into four parts. During Plebe Summer, all fourth classmen must learn the basics of sailing and seamanship. Later, the Command and Seamanship Training Squadron (CSTS) under the Division of Professional Development gives midshipmen the opportunity to put classroom lessons in seamanship to practical use. The intercollegiate team in small boats and the varsity offshore team complete the program. Approximately sixty midshipmen compete in one- and two-person boats on the intercollegiate team, and Navy consistently wins major national championships. The offshore team represents Navy in civilian competition all along the East Coast. In 1992, a Navy team for the first time won the prestigious Newport-to-Bermuda race, a feat comparable to an amateur baseball team winning the World Series.

As former Navy Sailing Director Captain John B. Bonds said, "We send them [midshipmen] to sea to learn the fundamental characteristic of the professional seaman; a deep-seated sense of humility in the face of nature and her master." And just like their nineteenth-century predecessors, midshipmen of today brave the power of the sea armed only with wind and sail.

Army-Navy Football Scores

Year	Score		Field	Year	Score		Field
1890	Navy 24	Army 0	West Point	1939	Navy 10	Army 0	Philadelphia Memorial Stadium
1891	Army 32	Navy 16	Annapolis	1940	Navy 14	Army 0	Philadelphia Memorial Stadium
1892	Navy 12	Army 4	West Point	1941	Navy 14	Army 6	Philadelphia Memorial Stadium
1893	Navy 6	Army 4	Annapolis	1942	Navy 14	Army 0	Thompson Stadium (Annapolis)
1894	Not played			1943	Navy 13	Army 0	Michie Stadium (West Point)
1895	Not played			1944	Army 23	Navy 7	Baltimore Stadium
1896	Not played			1945	Army 32	Navy 13	Philadelphia Memorial Stadium
1897	Not played			1946	Army 21	Navy 18	Philadelphia Memorial Stadium
1898	Not played			1947	Army 21	Navy 0	Philadelphia Memorial Stadium
1899	Army 17	Navy 5	Franklin Field (Philadelphia)	1948	Navy 21	Army 21	Philadelphia Memorial Stadium
1900	Navy 11	Army 7	Franklin Field	1949	Army 38	Navy 0	Philadelphia Memorial Stadium
1901	Army 11	Navy 5	Franklin Field	1950	Navy 14	Army 2	Philadelphia Memorial Stadium
1902	Army 22	Navy 8	Franklin Field	1951	Navy 42	Army 7	Philadelphia Memorial Stadium
1903	Army 40	Navy 5	Franklin Field	1952	Navy 7	Army 0	Philadelphia Memorial Stadium
1904	Army 11	Navy 0	Franklin Field	1953	Army 20	Navy 7	Philadelphia Memorial Stadium
1905	Navy 6	Army 6	Princeton	1954	Navy 27	Army 20	Philadelphia Memorial Stadium
1906	Navy 10	Army 0	Franklin Field	1955	Army 14	Navy 6	Philadelphia Memorial Stadium
1907	Navy 6	Army 0	Franklin Field	1956	Navy 7	Army 7	Philadelphia Memorial Stadium
1908	Army 6	Navy 4	Franklin Field	1957	Navy 14	Army 0	Philadelphia Memorial Stadium
1909	Not played			1958	Army 22	Navy 6	Philadelphia Memorial Stadium
1910	Navy 3	Army 0	Franklin Field	1959	Navy 43	Army 12	Philadelphia Memorial Stadium
1911	Navy 3	Army 0	Franklin Field	1960	Navy 17	Army 12	Philadelphia Memorial Stadium
1912	Navy 6	Army 0	Franklin Field	1961	Navy 13	Army 7	Philadelphia Memorial Stadium
1913	Army 22	Navy 9	Polo Grounds (New York)	1962	Navy 34	Army 14	Philadelphia Memorial Stadium
1914	Army 20	Navy 0	Franklin Field	1963	Navy 21	Army 15	Philadelphia Memorial Stadium
1915	Army 14	Navy 0	Polo Grounds	1964	Army 11	Navy 8	JFK Stadium (Philadelphia)
1916	Army 15	Navy 7	Polo Grounds	1965	Navy 7	Army 7	JFK Stadium
1917	Not played			1966	Army 20	Navy 7	JFK Stadium
1918	Not played			1967	Navy 19	Army 14	JFK Stadium
1919	Navy 6	Army 0	Polo Grounds	1968	Army 21	Navy 14	JFK Stadium
1920	Navy 7	Army 0	Polo Grounds	1969	Army 27	Navy 0	JFK Stadium
1921	Navy 7	Army 0	Polo Grounds				
1922	Army 17	Navy 14	Franklin Field				
1923	Navy 0	Army 0	Polo Grounds				
1924	Army 12	Navy 0	Baltimore Stadium				
1925	Army 10	Navy 3	Polo Grounds				
1926	Navy 21	Army 21	Soldier Field (Chicago)				
1927	Army 14	Navy 9	Polo Grounds				
1928	Not played						
1929	Not played						
1930	Army 6	Navy 0	Yankee Stadium (New York)				
1931	Army 17	Navy 7	Yankee Stadium				
1932	Army 20	Navy 0	Franklin Field				
1933	Army 12	Navy 7	Franklin Field				
1934	Navy 3	Army 0	Franklin Field				
1935	Army 28	Navy 6	Franklin Field				
1936	Navy 7	Army 0	Philadelphia Memorial Stadium				
1937	Army 6	Navy 0	Philadelphia Memorial Stadium				
1938	Army 14	Navy 7	Philadelphia Memorial Stadium				

Year	Score		Field
1970	Navy 11	Army 7	JFK Stadium
1971	Army 24	Navy 23	JFK Stadium
1972	Army 23	Navy 15	JFK Stadium
1973	Navy 51	Army 0	JFK Stadium
1974	Navy 19	Army 0	JFK Stadium
1975	Navy 30	Army 6	JFK Stadium
1976	Navy 38	Army 10	JFK Stadium
1977	Army 17	Navy 14	JFK Stadium
1978	Navy 28	Army 0	JFK Stadium
1979	Navy 31	Army 7	JFK Stadium
1980	Navy 33	Army 6	Veterans Stadium (Philadelphia)
1981	Navy 3	Army 3	Veterans Stadium
1982	Navy 24	Army 7	Veterans Stadium
1983	Navy 42	Army 13	Rose Bowl (Pasadena CA)
1984	Army 28	Navy 11	Veterans Stadium
1985	Navy 17	Army 7	Veterans Stadium
1986	Army 27	Navy 7	Veterans Stadium
1987	Army 17	Navy 3	Veterans Stadium
1988	Army 20	Navy 15	Veterans Stadium
1989	Navy 19	Army 17	Giants Stadium (East Rutherford, NJ)
1990	Army 30	Navy 20	Veterans Stadium
1991	Navy 24	Army 3	Veterans Stadium
1992	Army 25	Navy 24	Veterans Stadium
1993	Army 16	Navy 14	Giants Stadium

Navy Football First-Team All-Americas

Year Selected	Player, Class Year	Position
1907	Bill Dague, 1908	End
1908	Ed Lange, 1909	Quarterback
	Percy Northcroft, 1909	Tackle
1911	Jack Dalton, 1912	Fullback
1913	John "Babe" Brown, 1914	Guard
1917	Ernest Von Heimburg, 1919	End
1918	Lyman "Pop" Perry, 1920	Guard
	Wolcott Roberts, 1920	Halfback
1922	Wendell Taylor, 1923	End
1926	Tom Hamilton, 1927	Halfback
	Frank Wickhorst, 1927	Tackle
1928	Eddie Burke, 1934	Guard
1934	Fred "Buzz" Borries, 1935	Halfback
	Slade Cutter, 1935	Tackle
1943	George Brown, 1945	Guard
	Don Whitmire, 1947	Tackle
1944	Ben Chase, 1946	Guard
	Bobby Jenkins, 1947	Halfback
	Don Whitmire, 1947	Tackle
1945	Dick Duden, 1947	End
	Dick Scott, 1948	Center
1947	Dick Scott, 1948	Center

Year Selected	Player, Class Year	Position
1952	Steve Eisenhauer, 1954	Guard
1953	Steve Eisenhauer, 1954	Guard
1954	Ron Beagle, 1956	End
1955	Ron Beagle, 1956	End
1957	Bob Reifsnyder, 1959	Tackle
	Tom Forrestal, 1958	Quarterback
1960	Joe Bellino, 1961	Halfback
1961	Greg Mather, 1962	End
1963	Roger Staubach, 1965	Quarterback
1975	Chet Moeller, 1976	Defensive Back
1983	Napoleon McCallum, 1985	Halfback
1985	Napoleon McCallum, 1985	Halfback

Heisman Trophy Winners

1960	Joe Bellino, 1961	Halfback
1963	Roger Staubach, 1965	Quarterback

Maxwell Trophy Winners

1954	Ron Beagle, 1956	End
1957	Bob Reifsnyder, 1959	Tackle
1960	Joe Bellino, 1961	Halfback
1963	Roger Staubach, 1965	Quarterback

Academic All-Americas in Football

1953	Steve Eisenhauer, 1954	Guard
1957	Tom Forrestal, 1958	Quarterback
1958	Joe Tranchini, 1960	Quarterback
1969	Daniel Lee Pike, 1970	Running Back
1980	Theodore Dumbauld, 1981	Linebacker

National Football Foundation Gold Medal Recipients

1970	Tom Hamilton, 1927	Halfback
1979	Bill Lawrence, 1951	Back
1990	Tom Moorer, 1933	Tackle

National Collegiate Athletic Association Theodore Roosevelt Award Winners

1976	Tom Hamilton, 1927	Halfback
1984	Bill Lawrence, 1951	Back

Commander-in-Chief's Trophy Winners

Year	Winner
1972	Army
1973	Navy
1974	No winner (retained by Navy)
1975	Navy
1976	No winner (retained by Navy)
1977	Army
1978	Navy
1979	Navy
1980	No winner (retained by Navy)

Year	Winner
1981	Navy
1982	Air Force
1983	Air Force
1984	Army
1985	Air Force
1986	Army
1987	Air Force
1988	Army
1989	Air Force
1990	Air Force
1991	Air Force
1992	Air Force
1993	No winner (retained by Air Force)

National Football Foundation Hall of Fame Honorees

Year Selected	Player, Class Year	Position	Years Played
1953	John "Babe" Brown, 1914	Guard	1910–13
1956	Donald B. Whitmire, 1947	Tackle	1943–44
1960	Fred "Buzz" Borries, 1935	Halfback	1932–34
1965	Tom Hamilton, 1927	Quarterback	1924–26
1967	Slade Cutter, 1935	Tackle	1932–34
1968	Jonas Ingram, 1907	Fullback	1906
1970	Frank Wickhorst, 1927	Tackle	1924–26
	Jack Dalton, 1912	Fullback	1908–11
1971	Clyde "Smackover" Scott, 1949*	Halfback	1944–45
1973	William "Navy Bill" Ingram, 1920	Halfback	1916–18
1977	Joe Bellino, 1961	Halfback	1958–60
1981	Roger Staubach, 1965	Quarterback	1962–64
1985	George Brown, 1945	Guard	1942–43
	Anthony "Skip" Minisi, 1949*	Halfback	1945
1986	Ron Beagle, 1956	End	1953–55
1987	Dick Scott, 1948	Center	1945–47

*Non-graduate

Bowl Games

Date	Bowl	Place	Score
Jan. 1, 1924	Rose Bowl	Pasadena, Ca.	Navy 14 / Washington 14
Jan. 1, 1955	Sugar Bowl	New Orleans, La.	Navy 21 / Mississippi 0
Jan. 1, 1958	Cotton Bowl	Dallas, Tex.	Navy 20 / Rice 7
Jan. 2, 1961	Orange Bowl	Miami, Fla.	Missouri 21 / Navy 14
Jan. 1, 1964	Cotton Bowl	Dallas, Tex.	Texas 28 / Navy 6
Dec. 22, 1978	Holiday Bowl	San Diego, Ca.	Navy 23 / Brigham Young 16
Dec. 14, 1980	Garden State Bowl	E. Rutherford, N.J.	Houston 35 / Navy 0
Dec. 30, 1981	Liberty Bowl	Memphis, Tenn.	Ohio State 31 / Navy 28

Professional Athletes from the Naval Academy

Player, Class Year	Highest Rank	Team, Years
Wolcott Roberts, 1920	Ensign	N.A.
Frederick Denfeld, 1922 (did not graduate)	Commander (Naval Reserve)	N.A.
Art Carney, 1924	Midshipman	New York Giants, 1925–26
Bobby Orr Mathews, 1924	Rear Admiral	N.A.
Jim Schuber, 1928	Ensign	Chicago Bears
Ben Chase, 1946	Ensign, Lieutenant (Naval Reserve)	Detroit Lions, 1947
Jack Martin, 1946	Ensign	Los Angeles Rams, 1947–49
Dick Duden, 1947	Lieutenant	New York Giants, 1949
Joe Bartos, 1948	Captain, USMC	Washington Redskins, 1950
Tony Minisi, 1949 (did not graduate*)		New York Giants, 1948
Clyde Scott, 1949 (did not graduate*)		Philadelphia Eagles
Bob Reifsnyder, 1959	Discharged	New York Titans, 1960–61
Joe Bellino, 1961	Lieutenant, Captain (Naval Reserve)	Boston Patriots, 1965–67
Roger Staubach, 1965	Lieutenant	Dallas Cowboys, 1969–79
Phil McConkey, 1979	Lieutenant	New York Giants, 1984–87 Phoenix Cardinals, 1989
Napoleon McCallum, 1985	Lieutenant	Los Angeles Raiders, 1986–
David Robinson, 1987	Ensign, Lieutenant (jg) (Naval Reserve)	San Antonio Spurs, 1989–

Records are incomplete. There might have been some Naval Academy players who played in the early years of the National Football League.

*Clyde Scott graduated from Arkansas and Tony Minisi from Penn.

Navy Olympic Medal Winners

Name, Class Year	Olympiad/Sport	Medal
Harris Laning, 1895	1912 Rifle	Bronze, U.S. team
Carl T. Osburn, 1907	1912 Rifle	Bronze, U.S. team (high scorer)
		Silver, individual, Army rifle, 600 m
		Silver, individual, Army rifle, 300 m
		Bronze, U.S. team, miniature rifle, 50 m
Willis A. Lee, 1908	1920 Rifle	Gold, U.S. Military Team, 300 m prone
		Gold, U.S. team, 300 & 600 m prone
		Gold, U.S. team, 600 m prone
		Gold, U.S. team, any rifle
		Gold, U.S. team, miniature rifle, 50 m
		Silver, U.S. team, 300 m standing
		Bronze, U.S. team, single running deer
Carl T. Osburn, 1907	1920 Rifle	Gold, individual Army rifle, 300 m standing
		Gold, U.S. Military Team, 300 m prone
		Gold, U.S. team, 300 & 600 m prone
		Gold, U.S. team, any rifle
		Gold, U.S. team, 300 & 600 m prone
		Silver, U.S. team, 300 m standing
		Bronze, U.S. team, single running deer
Claiborne J. Walker,	1920 Fencing	Bronze, U.S. 1921A team, foils
Eight-Oared Crew Team	1920 Rowing	Gold, U.S. team
Sherman R. Clark, 1922		Coxswain
Clyde W. King, 1922		Stroke
Edwin D. Graves, 1921A		No. 2 (crew captain)
William C. Jordan, 1922		No. 3
Edward P. Moore, 1921B		No. 4
Alden R. Sanborn, 1922		No. 5
Donald H. Johnston, 1922		No. 6
Vincent J. Gallagher, Jr., 1922		No. 7
Virgil V. Jacomini, 1921A		Bow

Name, Class Year	Olympiad/Sport	Medal
Carl T. Osburn, 1907	1924 Rifle	Silver, individual, 600 m
Walter R. Stokes, 1922 (did not graduate)	1924 Rifle	Gold, U.S. team, 400, 600, 800 m
		Bronze, U.S. team, single running deer
George C. Calnan, 1920	1932 fencing	Bronze, U.S. team, foils
		Bronze, U.S. team, épée
Curtis Shears, 1932	1932 Fencing	Bronze, U.S. team, foils
Richard C. Steere, 1931	1932 Fencing	Bronze, U.S. team, foils
Raymond H. Bass, 1931	1932 Gymnastics	Gold, rope climb
Thomas F. Connelly, 1933	1932 Gymnastics	Bronze, rope climb
William T. Denton, 1933	1932 Gymnastics	Silver, rings
William Galbraith, 1929	1932 Gymnastics	Silver, rope climb
Robert E. Cowell, 1947	1948 Swimming	Silver, 100-m backstroke
Eight-Oared Crew Team	1952 Rowing	Gold, U.S. team
Charles D. Manring, 1952		Coxswain
Edward G. Stevens, Jr., 1954		Stroke
William B. Fields, 1954		No. 2
James R. Dunbar, 1955		No. 3
Richard F. Murphy, 1954		No. 4
Robert M. Detweiler, 1953		No. 5
Henry A. Proctor, 1954		No. 6
Wayne T. Frye, 1954		No. 7
Frank B. Shakespeare, 1953		Bow
Josiah Henson, 1945	1952 Wrestling	Bronze, 136½ lbs.
Peter S. Blair, 1955	1956 Wrestling	Bronze, 191 lbs.
Lloyd W. Keaser, 1972	1976 Wrestling	Silver, 149½ lbs. freestyle
David Robinson, 1987	1988 Basketball	Bronze
David Robinson, 1987	1992 Basketball	Gold
Brian Ledbetter, 1985	1992 Yachting	Silver, Finn Class

CHAPTER EIGHT

ANNAPOLIS:
The Academy's Home Port

From the very beginning, strong ties have always existed between the Naval Academy and the town of Annapolis. Franklin Buchanan married Ann Catharine Lloyd in 1835 at the Chase-Lloyd House on Maryland Avenue ten years before he became the Academy's first superintendent. His bride belonged to a prominent local family, and her father had twice been elected governor of the state. When the Naval School opened its doors in 1845, the Buchanans saw to it that the midshipmen were received into Annapolitan society.

In fact, Annapolis was delighted to have been selected as the home of the Naval School. The town fathers hoped to revitalize what had once been the thriving port of entry to the Chesapeake Bay. Founded in the mid-1600s as Providence, it became Anne Arundel Town and then Annapolis in honor of Princess Anne of England when it was named provincial capital in 1694. Under the direction of its governor, Sir Francis Nicholson, the city was laid out in a Baroque plan. Streets radiated from two central circles. State Circle, the seat of the Maryland legislature, was purposely built larger and on higher ground than Church Circle to symbolize the supremacy of the state over the church. Because Annapolis was Maryland's capital and a bustling port, it attracted wealthy merchants and statesmen who built elegant homes in the Georgian and Federal styles. Four of these homes were owned by Samuel Chase, Charles Carroll, William Paca, and Thomas Stone, the only four Marylanders to sign the Declaration of Independence. This was Annapolis's golden age.

Indeed, Annapolis played an important role in the colonies' movement toward freedom from England. The Sons of Liberty, led by Chase and Paca, met beneath the Liberty Tree on the grounds of King William's School, later Saint John's College. In an incident similar to the Boston Tea Party, the brig *Peggy Stewart* was burned off Windmill Point, where the Academy now stands, to protest the despised tax on the tea she was carrying. Although Annapolis saw no action in the war itself, the Continental Congress met in the Maryland State House on State Circle from November 1783 through August 1784. During this period, Annapolis served as the capital of the United States, and in the Old Senate Chamber of the State House, General George Washington set an important precedent for the new nation. Refusing to become king or military dictator, he resigned his commission as commander in chief of the Continental Army and returned the government to the people. Three weeks later, on January 14, 1784, Congress, meeting again in the Old Senate Chamber, ratified the Treaty of Paris and formally ended the Revolutionary War.

Alumni House, formerly Ogle Hall, was the residence of Samuel Ogle and a number of other Maryland governors. This two-story Georgian brick structure was also home to the descendants of Admiral David Dixon Porter, superintendent of the Naval Academy from 1865 to 1869. In 1944, Admiral Porter's granddaughter sold the house to the Naval Academy Alumni Association, for which it now serves as headquarters.

Historic Middleton Tavern at City Dock dates from the mid-eighteenth century. It was owned for years by Horatio Middleton and his descendants, who also ran a ferry between Annapolis and the Eastern Shore.

The USNA Chapel dome is seen from the restored gardens of the William Paca House. From 1907 to 1965, the paved-over gardens served as a parking lot for Carvel Hall Hotel. In its heyday, Carvel Hall was the center of social life for both the Academy and Annapolis.

Maryland Avenue, leading from State Circle to the Academy gate, has always been a magnet for midshipmen. Known in the late nineteenth century as Robbers' Row, the street tempted many a midshipman to overspend his meager pay on tantalizing goods displayed in store windows.

Although Annapolis continued to be the seat of the Maryland legislature, by the early nineteenth century it could no longer claim to be the principal port on the Chesapeake. Baltimore, with its deeper harbor, had eclipsed Annapolis, and the town's economy began a steady decline. However, the lack of development had the result of leaving Annapolis an almost perfectly preserved eighteenth-century town, since few buildings were torn down to make way for new construction.

In hopes of revitalizing the business community, the Maryland Assembly, beginning in 1826, undertook an active campaign to attract a naval school to its shores. When the Academy was finally established in 1845, Annapolitans welcomed the faculty and students with great enthusiasm.

Secretary of the Navy George Bancroft was equally enthusiastic about the location. He was anxious to consolidate the Navy's four shore-based schools into one and to remove midshipmen from the big-city temptations of New York, Boston, Philadelphia, and Norfolk. The small, provincial town of Annapolis provided the ideal setting. Even then, the authorities made sure that an enclosing wall divided the School from the town in order to isolate the midshipmen from the distractions so close at hand.

Nevertheless, it proved impossible to separate Annapolis and the Academy completely. The streets of town led directly to the Academy gates, and the shops and taverns proved irresistible to the midshipmen. They gathered together after hours to drink rum punches and eat oyster pies at such establishments as Rosey's and Dauté's taverns, and in their few hours of liberty, they patronized the merchants just outside the main gate. Many a midshipman overspent his meager pay on the tantalizing goods displayed in the windows of stores along Maryland Avenue, known as Robbers' Row. Shopkeepers were more than happy to offer liberal credit against a midshipman's income after graduation. Over time, some midshipmen ran up such extensive debts that it took them years to repay their creditors. Finally, Academy officials instituted a policy requiring that all debts be paid before a midshipman could be graduated.

Various establishments grew up to serve the needs of midshipmen and officers attached to the Academy. At one time a dozen tailor shops on Maryland Avenue alone specialized in fitting naval uniforms. Just as the town fathers had hoped, the Academy's presence brought renewal to the business community and the life of the town.

Through the years, the presence of the midshipmen has added much to the character of Annapolis. Just three months after its founding, the Naval School hosted a formal ball, which was held annually thereafter. Midshipmen became an important part of the social life of the town. As one of them wrote home, he and his fellows were received with the courtesies usually accorded only to the highest ranking officers. The young ladies of Annapolis were naturally delighted to have so many eligible young men in residence, and from time to time newly commissioned officers married their local sweethearts, further cementing their ties with the town.

After the Civil War, social life at the Academy flourished under Superintendent David Dixon Porter. In his time, Sunday afternoons brought scores of visitors to the Academy grounds. Midshipmen escorted their girls down the tree-lined walks or treated them to a sail on the Severn. As it became easier to travel to Annapolis, midshipmen began to invite their steadies from home down for the weekend. Many of the inns and lodgings in town housed the "drags" and became known as drag houses.

From 1907 to 1965, those midshipmen who could afford it put their girls up at Carvel Hall, an elegant two-hundred-room hotel built on the old gardens of William Paca's house. Even the poorest midshipmen saved for months so that they could dine with their dates at the hotel. In its heyday, Carvel Hall was the center of social life for both the Academy and Annapolis. Sooner or later, everyone in town passed through its doors. The doorman himself held sway over his domain, and several who had this position over the years became local celebrities. One old retainer from the 1920s boasted that he had been at his post so long that he addressed every admiral by his first name, having known them all as young midshipmen. When Carvel Hall was torn down in 1965, Historic Annapolis restored the original Paca House and reconstructed the lovely gardens that had been covered over by the hotel and parking lot.

As the Academy grew over the years, its ties to Annapolis became even stronger. More and more faculty members made the town their home, and it seemed as if someone connected with the Academy lived on every block. Townspeople rallied behind the midshipmen and became staunch supporters of the athletic teams. In the days when the regiment traveled to the Army-Navy game by train, avid fans would rise before dawn and stand on their porches in bathrobes and nightclothes to wish the midshipmen good luck as they marched by to the station. For many seasons, midshipmen could count on seeing Professor Cusacks, who taught French at the Acade-

Dressed in the style of the eighteenth century, guides from Historic Annapolis lead tours of the town and the Naval Academy. More than four million people visit Annapolis annually and explore the town, which was planned by colonial governor Sir Francis Nicholson.

my. He and his two beautiful daughters were always on their front lawn cheering the midshipmen on their way to the big game, no matter how early the hour.

The churches in town provided another link with the Academy. Up until the mid-1970s, Sunday morning chapel was mandatory, but midshipmen could choose to attend churches in town if they preferred not to participate in the service at the Academy. Annapolis residents fondly recall watching the "church parties" on their way to worship, and the local congregations warmly welcomed the young men. Many friendships developed, and some families invited midshipmen into their homes and offered them a brief respite from the rigors of Academy life. To give all midshipmen a chance to enjoy such a home away from home, the Academy introduced a sponsor program in the 1950s that matched midshipmen and local families. Many developed strong ties with their sponsors and have kept in touch with them over the years from duty stations throughout the world.

Just as the townspeople have given much to the midshipmen, midshipmen in turn have given much back to the community. They have always been ready to help out in emergencies, and many times were called on to join the bucket brigade to fight fires in town. During one major fire in the late 1870s, the battalion fought so bravely that Superintendent Foxhall Parker rewarded them with extra privileges. Today, the midshipmen perform countless hours of community service, tutoring local schoolchildren, collecting food for the needy, and rehabilitating homes for the elderly.

The town of Annapolis and the Naval Academy have, with few exceptions, lived happily side by side for over one hundred and fifty years. Like close relations, midshipmen and townspeople share good times and bad and gather together to celebrate special days throughout the year. They come to Farragut Field to view the fireworks on the Fourth of July. In December, they stand at the seawall to watch the Christmas Parade of Lights sail by on the water. On summer evenings, they listen to the Naval Academy Band as it plays sunset serenades from the City Dock. And when the brigade marches in precise formation in dress parades on Worden Field, Annapolitans and Academy officials alike take pride in the young men and women who proudly wear the blue and gold.

Thomas Point Lighthouse on the South River just outside Annapolis.

The oldest state capitol in continuous legislative use, the Maryland State House was the first peacetime capitol of the nation. In the old Senate Chamber, General George Washington resigned his commission as commander in chief of the Continental Army on December 23, 1783. Three weeks later, in the same chamber, Congress ratified the Treaty of Paris, formally ending the Revolutionary War.

USNA ALUMNI MEDAL OF HONOR AWARDS

The Navy Medal of Honor, awarded "in the name of the Congress of the United States," was established by law on 21 December 1861—the first decoration formally authorized by the American Government to be worn as a badge of honor—for enlisted men of the Navy and Marine Corps. The Army Medal of Honor was established on 17 February 1862, but the act was amended on 3 March 1863 to include officers and to make the award retroactive to the beginning of the Civil War. However, it was not until 3 March 1915 that the Navy law was amended to provide eligibility for the Medal of Honor to officers of the Navy, Marine Corps, and Coast Guard. The first such awards—27 in all—were made to those officers who had distinguished themselves during the landings and occupation of Vera Cruz, Mexico, in April 1914, when no other medal for gallantry had been established.

The list includes ranks at the time, name, USNA Class, occasion for the award, and final rank in which serving or retired. Asterisks indicate posthumous awards.

Capt. (RAdm.) Edwin Alexander Anderson USN, 1882, Vera Cruz, Apr. 1914

Cdr. (RAdm.) Richard Nott Antrim USN, 1931, Japanese POW Camp, Apr. 1942

Ens. (Adm.) Oscar Charles Badger USN, 1911, Vera Cruz, Apr. 1914

*LCol. Harold William Bauer USMC, 1930, Guadalcanal Air Operations, 1942

*Capt. Mervyn Sharp Bennion USN, 1910, USS *West Virginia*, 7 Dec. 1941

Cdr. (Capt.) Willis Winter Bradley, Jr. USN, 1907, Ammo. Explosion, USS *PITTSBURGH*, 23 July 1917, Member of Congress, 1947

LCdr. (Capt.) Allen Buchanan USN, 1899, Vera Cruz, Apr. 1914

LCdr. (RAdm.) John Duncan Bulkeley USN, 1933, Dec. 1941–Apr. 1942, Philippines

Cdr. (RAdm.) Richard Evelyn Byrd USN (Ret.), 1912, Polar Exploration (Special Legislation 1927)

*RAdm. Daniel Judson Callaghan USN, 1911, Second Battle of Savo, 12–13 Nov. 1942

Ens. (RAdm.) Robert Webster Cary, Jr. USN, 1914, Boiler Explosion, USS *SAN DIEGO*, 21 Jan. 1915

Lt. (Cdr.) Guy Wilkinson Stuart Castle USN, 1901, Vera Cruz, Apr. 1914

Maj. (BGen.) Albertus Wright Catlin USMC, 1890, Vera Cruz, Apr. 1914

*LCdr. William Merrill Corry, Jr. USN, 1910, Rescued pilots from air crash, 2 Oct. 1920

Lt. (jg) (Cdr.) George McCall Courts USN, 1907, Vera Cruz, Apr. 1914

*Capt. John Philip Cromwell USN, 1924, USS *Sculpin*, 19 Nov. 1943

*Cdr. George Fleming Davis USN, 1934, USS *Walke*, Lingayen Gulf, 6 Jan. 1945

*Cdr. Samuel David Dealey USN, 1930, USS *Harder*, Fifth War Patrol, 1944

*Ens. Henry Clay Drexler USN, 1924, Turret explosion, USS *TRENTON*, 20 Oct. 1924, (Special Legislation 1933)

LCdr. Walter Atlee Edwards USN, 1910, Sea rescue of 482 persons, 16 Dec. 1922

*Cdr. Ernest Edwin Evans USN, 1931, USS *Johnston*, Leyte Gulf, 25 Oct. 1944

RAdm. Frank Friday Fletcher USN, 1875, Vera Cruz, Apr. 1914

Lt. (Adm.) Frank Jack Fletcher USN, 1906, Vera Cruz, Apr. 1914

Cdr. (RAdm.) Eugene Bennett Fluckey USN, 1935, USS *Barb*, Eleventh Patrol, 1945

Ens. (VAdm.) Paul Frederick Foster USN, 1911, Vera Cruz, Apr. 1914

Ens. (Cdr.) Hugh Carroll Frazer USN, 1912, Vera Cruz, Apr. 1914

LCdr. (RAdm.) Samuel Glenn Fuqua USN, 1923, USS *Arizona*, 7 Dec. 1941

*Cdr. Howard Walter Gilmore USN, 1926, USS *Growler*, 7 Feb. 1943

Cdr. William Kelly Harrison USN, 1889, Vera Cruz, Apr. 1914

Lt. (RAdm.) Charles Conway Hartigan USN, 1906, Vera Cruz, Apr. 1914

2nd Lt. (Col.) Harry Leroy Hawthorne USA, 1882, Wounded Knee Creek, S.D., 29 Dec. 1890, (Army medal awarded under law of 3 Mar. 1863)

Lt. (RAdm.) Richmond Pearson Hobson USN, 1898, USS *Merrimac*, Cuba, 3 June 1898, (Special Legislation 1933), Member of Congress 1907–15

Lt. (jg) (Capt.) Thomas Jerome Hudner, Jr. USN, 1947, Chosin Reservoir, Korea, 4 Dec. 1950

Capt. (VAdm.) Harry McLaren Pinckney Huse USN, 1878, Vera Cruz, Apr. 1914

*Lt. Carlton Barmore Hutchins USN, 1926, Saved crew landing damaged plane, 2 Feb. 1938

Lt. (jg) (Adm.) Jonas Howard Ingram USN, 1907, Vera Cruz, Apr. 1914

Lt. (LCdr.) Edouard Victor Michael Izac USN, 1915, POW German U-90, 21 May 1918, Member of Congress, 1937

Lt. (RAdm.) Rufus Zenas Johnston USN, 1895, Vera Cruz, Apr. 1914

Cdr. (RAdm.) Claud Ashton Jones USN, 1907, Wreck of USS *MEMPHIS*, 29 Aug. 1916

*RAdm. Isaac Campbell Kidd USN, 1906, USS *Arizona*, 7 Dec. 1941

Lt. (RAdm.) James Patrick Lannon USN, 1902, Vera Cruz, Apr. 1914

*1st Lt. Baldomero Lopez USMC, 1948, Inchon, Korea, 15 Sept. 1950

Ens. (RAdm.) George Maus Lowry USN, 1911, Vera Cruz, Apr. 1914

Cdr. (Capt.) David McCampbell USN, 1933, Air Ops. Philippine Sea, June 1944

Cdr. (RAdm.) Bruce McCandless USN, 1932, USS *San Francisco*, 12–13 Nov. 1942

Lt. (Capt.) Richard Miles McCool, Jr. USN, 1945, Ryukus Landing, June 1945

Ens. (VAdm.) Edward Orrick McDonnell USN, 1912, Vera Cruz, Apr. 1914

Lt. (Capt.) Frederick Vallette McNair, Jr. USN, 1903, Vera Cruz, Apr. 1914

Cdr. (RAdm.) William Adger Moffett USN, 1890, Vera Cruz, Apr. 1914

Lt. Col. (MGen.) Wendell Cushing Neville USMC, 1890, Vera Cruz, Apr. 1914, Commandant USMC 1929–30

Lt. (LCdr.) Edward Henry O'Hare USN, 1937, Aerial Combat, 20 Feb. 1942

Cdr. (RAdm.) Richard Hetherington O'Kane USN, 1934, USS *Tang*, 23–24 Oct. 1944

*Lt. John James Powers USN, 1935, Coral Sea, 9 May 1942

Cdr. (VAdm.) Lawson Paterson Ramage USN, 1931, USS *Parche*, 31 July 1944

*2nd Lt. Robert Dale Reem USMC, 1948, Korea, 6 Nov. 1950

*Lt. Milton Ernest Ricketts USN, 1935, USS *Yorktown*, Coral Sea, 8 May 1942

*Capt. Albert Harold Rooks USN, 1914, USS *Houston*, Java Sea, Feb. 1942

Capt. William Rees Rush USN, 1877, Vera Cruz, Apr. 1914

Ens. (RAdm.) Thomas J. Ryan USN, 1921, Rescue operations, Japanese earthquake, 1923

Cdr. (RAdm.) Herbert Emery Schonland USN, 1925, USS *San Francisco*, 12–13 Nov. 1942

*RAdm. Norman Scott USN, 1911, Second Battle Savo, 12–13 Nov. 1942

F1 / c (Midn.) D. Henry Lakin Simpson, 1882, USS *Essex*, 31 Oct. 1877

Lt. (RAdm.) Adolphus Staton USN, 1902, Vera Cruz, Apr. 1914

Cdr. (RAdm.) Herman Osman Stickney USN, 1888, Vera Cruz, Apr. 1914

Capt. (VAdm.) James B. Stockdale USN, 1947, North Vietnam, 4 Sept. 1969

Cdr. (Capt.) George Levick Street III USN, 1937, USS *Tirante*, Apr. 1945

Lt. (RAdm.) Julius Curtis Townsend USN, 1902, Vera Cruz, Apr. 1914

*Capt. Franklin Van Valkenburgh USN, 1909, USS *Arizona*, 7 Dec. 1941

*LCdr. Bruce Avery Van Voorhis USN, 1929, Solomon Islands, 6 July 1943

Lt. (Cdr.) Richard Wainwright, Jr. USN, 1902, Vera Cruz, Apr. 1914

Ens. (VAdm.) Theodore Stark Wilkinson, Jr. USN, 1909, Vera Cruz, Apr. 1914

Cdr. (Capt.) Cassin Young USN, 1916, USS *Vestal*, 7 Dec. 1941

Following pages: On display in Preble Hall is a complete collection of Naval Academy class rings dating back to the first in 1869. The rings are part of the 50,000-item museum collection which also includes the Beverly R. Robinson naval prints, ship models, battle flags, and other naval artifacts and trophies.

NOTES

Chapter One

The quotations in this chapter, in order of appearance, come from the following sources:

"The atmosphere seems . . ." Duval, Ruby R. "Perpetuation of History and Tradition . . ." p. 139.

"by requiring . . ." McKee, Kinnaird R., Admiral. Report on USNA academics, p. 3.

"I can imagine . . ." *Lucky Bag,* 1967, p. 85.

Chapter Two

The following sources were used extensively in this chapter:

Benjamin, Park. *The United States Naval Academy.*

Bolander, Louis H. "A Hundred Years of the Naval Academy."

————. "The Naval Academy in Five Wars."

"The First Academic Staff." *Proceedings,* October 1935.

Ford, Thomas G. "History of the United States Naval Academy."

Lovette, Leland P. *School of the Sea.*

"One Hundredth Anniversary of the Naval Academy." *Shipmate,* October 1945.

Sturdy, Henry Francis. "The Founding of the Naval Academy by Bancroft and Buchanan."

Sweetman, Jack. *The U.S. Naval Academy.*

The quotations in this chapter, in order of appearance, come from the following sources:

"The want of a naval school . . ." President John Quincy Adams quoted in Henry Francis Sturdy's "The Founding of the Naval Academy . . ." p. 1368.

"applications, zeal . . ." Commander Franklin Buchanan quoted in Sturdy, p. 1373.

"his energy, zeal . . ." Commander Franklin Buchanan quoted in "The First Academic Staff," p. 1398.

"wretched ramshackle." Lovette. *School of the Sea,* p. 56.

"As dissipation . . ." Commander Franklin Buchanan quoted in Sturdy, p. 1374.

"for repairs . . ." Commander Franklin Buchanan quoted in Park Benjamin's *The United States Naval Academy,* p. 168.

"The youngsters . . ." Benjamin, p. 182.

"would rather go . . ." Ford. "History of the United States Naval Academy," chapter 13, p. 25.

"our Certificates . . ." Petition of first classmen quoted in Ford, chapter 16, p. 1.

"Resign or . . ." Telegram from W. L. Yancey quoted in Ford, chapter 16, p. 2.

"stick by 'The Old Flag' . . ." Robley D. Evans quoted in Felix Riesenberg's *The Story of the Naval Academy,* pp. 55–56.

"is not defensible . . ." Letter of Superintendent G. S. Blake to Secretary of the Navy, April 15, 1861.

"Thank God . . ." Exchange between Superintendent G. S. Blake and General Benjamin Butler quoted in Benjamin, p. 231.

"Be true . . ." Commandant C. R. P. Rodgers quoted in Ford, chapter 16, pp. 30–31.

"sustained the reputation . . ." Commander Samuel Dupont quoted in Ford, chapter 18, pp. 37–38.

"return of . . ." Ford, chapter 19, p. 28.

"The long row . . ." Magruder, P. H. "The U.S. Naval Academy and Annapolis . . ." p. 72.

"At this time . . ." Letter from an Army officer quoted in Walter Aamold's "Athletic Training at the Naval Academy," p. 1562.

"You may fire . . ." Admiral George Dewey quoted in Kenneth J. Hagan's *This People's Navy,* pp. 220.

"The fleet under . . ." Rear Admiral William T. Sampson quoted in Hagan, p. 225.

"It had been a strange war . . ." A Naval Academy instructor quoted in Ken Kimble's "Spanish Prisoners in Annapolis."

Chapter Three

The following sources were used extensively in this chapter:

Bolander, Louis H. "A Hundred Years of the Naval Academy."

———. "The Naval Academy in Five Wars."

Hagan, Kenneth J. *This People's Navy.*

Hough, Richard. *The Great Admirals.*

Lovette, Leland P. *School of the Sea.*

Mersky, Peter B., and Polmar, Norman. *The Naval Air War in Vietnam.*

Morison, Samuel Eliot. *The Oxford History of the American People.*

"One Hundredth Anniversary of the Naval Academy." *Shipmate,* October 1945.

Santoli, Al. *Everything We Had.*

Spector, Ronald H. *Eagle Against the Sun.*

Sweetman, Jack. *The U.S. Naval Academy.*

Uhlig, Frank, Jr. *Vietnam, The Naval Story.*

The quotations in this chapter, in order of appearance, come from the following sources:

"This escapade . . ." Admiral Chester W. Nimitz quoted in E. B. Potter's *Nimitz,* p. 55.

"The Navy took 'em . . ." Foley, Francis, ed., *Army-Navy Fire,* 1930, p. 51.

"Superintendent Willson was called . . ." Captain William S. Busik quoted in Dino W. Buchanan's and Tami Terella's "Mids, grads, locals recall vivid memories of Pearl Harbor." *Trident,* December 6, 1991, p. 1.

"The scariest thing . . ." Busik, William S., Captain. Interview with authors, February 3, 1992.

"you couldn't have won . . ." James V. Forrestal quoted in "Through Five Wars." *Shipmate,* October 1945, p. 85.

"It was the first time . . ." Carter, Jimmy. *Why Not the Best?,* p. 59.

"deliberately inflicted . . ." Stockdale Medal of Honor Citation.

"The Naval Academy is . . ." Lawrence, William P., Vice Admiral. Letter to editor, *Washington Magazine,* January 1980, p. 20.

"The Academy . . ." Calvert, James F., Vice Admiral. *Superintendent's Report to Board of Visitors,* May 2, 1970, p. 29; May 12, 1972, p. 22.

Chapter Four

The following sources were used extensively in this chapter: interviews with graduates, midshipmen, and Academy personnel; letters, journals, and diaries; *Lucky Bags*; Oral Histories; *Reef Points*; and *Trident*s.

The quotations in this chapter, in order of appearance, come from the following sources:

"we have to show . . ." Heinz Lenz quoted in Tami Terella's " 'Good morning Class of 1995. It's time for PEP!' " *Trident,* July 26, 1991, p. 8.

"I've forgotten . . ." Joe Bellino quoted in Shirley Povich's "Dynamite Joe of Navy." *The Saturday Evening Post,* October 1, 1960, p. 90.

"because they're eventually . . ." Plebe sailing instructor quoted in Tami Terella's "Plebe Summer Sailing Program sets course." *Trident,* July 10, 1992, p. 5.

"The acrid fumes . . ." *Lucky Bag,* 1942, p. 409.

"Sweat, sweat . . ." Plebe. Interview with authors, September 11, 1992.

"Next year . . ." Plebe. Interview with authors, May 23, 1992.

"we thought . . ." Jurika, Stephen, Jr., Captain. *Oral History*, p. 43.

"It is axiomatic . . ." *Lucky Bag*, 1947, p. 12.

"By the time . . ." Haskell, Orin Shepley. Letter of December 2, 1918.

"The Academy takes away . . ." Graduate. Interview with authors, October 21, 1991.

"first class and kings . . ." *Lucky Bag*, 1949, p. 388.

"discovered hidden resources . . ." Kauffman, Draper L., Rear Admiral. *Oral History*, p. 79.

Chapter Five

The following sources were used extensively in this chapter: interviews with graduates, midshipmen, and Academy personnel; letters, journals, and diaries; *Lucky Bag*s; Oral Histories; *Reef Points*; and *Trident*s.

The quotations in this chapter, in order of appearance, come from the following sources:

"You can strive . . ." North, Oliver. *Under Fire*, p. 81.

"From the halls of Mother Bancroft . . ." Plebe. Interview with authors, September 11, 1992.

"If he had his mind . . ." Davidson, John F., Rear Admiral. *Oral History*, p. 13.

"Gentlemen, I have heard . . ." Superintendent Louis Nulton quoted in Vice Admiral William R. Smedberg III's *Oral History*, p. 17.

"The Academy makes you . . ." Napoleon McCallum quoted in Damaine Vonada's "Ohioans." *Ohio*, September 1984, p. 18.

"Mr. Nelson . . ." Professor Arsène Girault and Midshipman William Nelson quoted in Park Benjamin's *The United States Naval Academy*, p. 187.

"A messmate before . . ." Benjamin, p. 183.

"The character . . ." Admiral David Dixon Porter quoted in Thomas G. Ford's "History of the U.S. Naval Academy," chapter 20, p. 102.

"To the ladies . . ." Traditional song quoted in Ford, chapter 12, p. 5.

"knowing well . . ." Ford, chapter 14, p. 18.

"Went to the hop . . ." Davis, Ellsworth. Letter of November 17, 1912.

"just as starry-eyed . . ." Admiral James Holloway III quoted in Tami Terella's "Anniversary classes stroll down memory lane." *Trident*, October 23, 1992, p. 3.

Chapter Six

The following sources were used extensively in this chapter: interviews with graduates, midshipmen, and Academy personnel; letters, journals, and diaries; *Lucky Bag*s; Oral Histories; *Reef Points*; *Trident*s; and USNA Sports Information files.

The quotations in this chapter, in order of appearance, come from the following sources:

"When the fight . . ." *Reef Points*, 1933–34, p. 139.

"No more rivers . . ." Traditional chant quoted in Neil Borgquist Musser's *My Life at the U.S. Naval Academy*, p. 12.

"Yes, that's very true . . ." Kauffman, Draper L., Rear Admiral. *Oral History*, p. 28.

"The smoking lamp is lit." Graduate. Interview with authors, July 9, 1993.

"the [two] services . . ." Colonel Michael Hagee quoted in Tami Terella's "Mids learn, experience importance of 'Navy-Marine Corps team,'" *Trident*, August 9, 1991, p. 4.

"It is the best place . . ." McN., T. C. "After the Ball is Over." *Log Splinter*, May 15, 1953, p. 17.

"You can take . . ." Mother of Color Girl Barbara Engle quoted in "Tradition of the Color Girl." USNA Museum exhibit, spring 1992.

Chapter Seven

The following sources were used extensively in this chapter:
Aamold, Walter. "Athletic Training at the Naval Academy."

———. "Naval Academy Athletics."

Schoor, Gene. *100 Years of Army-Navy Football.*

Taylor, Craig E. "Fifty Years Ago Today—The 1926 Army-Navy Game." *Army-Navy Program*, 1976, pp. 102–125.

In addition, the following materials were also used extensively: interviews with graduates, midshipmen, and Academy personnel; letters, journals, and diaries; *Lucky Bag*s; Oral Histories; *Trident*s; and USNA Sports Information files and programs.

The quotations in this chapter, in order of appearance, come from the following sources:
"Most of all . . ." Midshipman quoted in Dianne Boyer's "Navy 'playmaker' attacks foes in match-stick games of challenge." *Trident*, May 3, 1991, p. 15.

"The Army-Navy game . . ." Jonas Ingram quoted in Rear Admiral Francis D. Foley's *Oral History*, p. 96.

"the rooms were so cold . . ." Aamold. "Athletic Training," p. 1564.

"Harry Truman had beaten . . ." Jack Clary quoted in Claire Smith's "Spirit remains, but game's not the same." Philadelphia *Bulletin* (n.d.).

"We were winning the game . . ." Midshipman quoted in "Victory in Philadelphia." *Trident*, December 13, 1991, p. 8.

"It is easy to pick . . ." President John F. Kennedy quoted in Jack Zanger's "Army vs. Navy." *Sport*, October 1969, p. 60.

"In my opinion . . ." Vice Admiral Robert B. Pirie quoted in Bill Sauder's "Webb Boxed Navy's Ears with Dignity." *Ledger-Star*, May 3, 1961.

"Boxing most easily . . ." Ratrie, Ellen Walker. "College boxing roots traced through Academy." *Trident*, February 15, 1991, p. 12.

"Keep your hands up . . ." Emerson Smith quoted in Oliver North's *Under Fire*, p. 82.

"Damn it, Carnevale . . ." General William Westmoreland quoted in Paul Stillwell's "Footballs Aweigh!" *Shipmate*, September, 1981, p. 46.

"Good players help . . ." David Robinson quoted in Eastman Kodak press release, March 24, 1987.

"You can keep . . ." Chant quoted in Clive Gammon's "A Wicket Championship," *Sports Illustrated*, May 25, 1987, p. 86.

"we send them . . ." Captain John B. Bonds quoted in Tami Terella's "Plebes learn basics of 'sailoring' through P–100 instruction." *Trident*, July 12, 1991, p. 3.

Chapter Eight

Most of the information in this chapter came from correspondence, interviews, *Lucky Bag*s, Oral Histories, tours, and *Trident*s.

SELECTED BIBLIOGRAPHY

Histories, Descriptions and General Sources

Aamold, Walter. "Athletic Training at the Naval Academy." *Proceedings* (U.S. Naval Institute), October 1935.

———. "Naval Academy Athletics—1845 to 1945." *Proceedings* (USNI), April 1946.

Banning, Kendall. *Annapolis Today.* 6th ed., Annapolis, Md.: U.S. Naval Institute, 1963.

Batchellor, Oliver Ambrose. "Correspondence of Oliver Ambrose Batchellor 1859–1865." USNA Nimitz Library, Special Collections, Annapolis, Md.

Bates, Thomas F. "The Army-Navy Series: 100 Years of Tradition." Navy Sports Information release, U.S. Naval Academy, Annapolis, Md., November 7, 1990.

———. "Navy Winning Streaks," Sports Information chart.

———. "USNA First Team Women All-Americas," chart compiled for authors, August 1993.

Benjamin, Park. *Shakings.* Boston: Lee & Shepard, 1868.

———. *The United States Naval Academy.* New York: G. P. Putnam Sons, 1900.

Bolander, Louis H. "A Hundred Years of the Naval Academy." *Proceedings* (USNI), April 1946.

———. "The Naval Academy in Five Wars." *Proceedings* (USNI), April 1946.

———. "The U.S. Naval Academy—Its First Proud Century." Baltimore *Sun, Sunday Magazine*, October 7, 1945.

Buchanan, Franklin, Commander. "Official Letter Book 1845–1847." USNA Nimitz Library, Special Collections, Annapolis, Md.

Carter, Jimmy. *Why Not the Best?* New York: Bantam, 1976.

Cope, Harley, Rear Admiral, and Captain Walter Karig. *Battle Submerged: Submarine Fighters of World War II.* New York: W. W. Norton, 1951.

Davis, Ellsworth. "Correspondence of Ellsworth Davis, 1907–1933." USNA Nimitz Library, Special Collections, Annapolis, Md.

Duval, Ruby R. "The Perpetuation of History and Tradition at the Century-Old U.S. Naval Academy." *Proceedings* (USNI), April 1946.

Edsall, Margaret Horton. *A Place Called the Yard.* Annapolis, Md.: D. W. E. and Associates, 1992.

Engeman, Jack. *Annapolis: The Life of a Midshipman.* New York: Lothrop, Lee & Shepard, 1956.

Fag Ends from the U.S. Naval Academy. New York: Homer Lee, 1878.

"The First Academic Staff." *Proceedings* (USNI), October 1935.

Folk, Winston, Lieutenant. "The Confederate States Naval Academy." *Proceedings* (USNI), September 1934.

Ford, Thomas G. "History of the U.S. Naval Academy." 1887. USNA Nimitz Library, Special Collections, Annapolis, Md.

Frank, Benis M. *Okinawa: The Great Island Battle.* New York: Elsevier-Dutton, 1978.

Hagan, Kenneth J. *This People's Navy.* New York: Free Press, 1991.

Haskell, Orin Shepley. "Correspondence of Orin Shepley Haskell, 1916–1918." USNA Nimitz Library, Special Collections, Annapolis, Md.

Holmes, Wilfred J., Captain. "Youngster Cruise Journal of Wilfred J. Holmes, 1919."

Hough, Richard. *The Great Admirals.* New York: William Morrow, 1977.

Hoyt, Edwin P. *Carrier Wars: Naval Aviation from World War II to the Persian Gulf.* New York: McGraw-Hill, 1989.

Kimble, Ken. "Spanish Prisoners in Annapolis." *The Publick Enterprise*, July, August 1989.

Log, various editions. USNA Nimitz Library, Special Collections, Annapolis, Md.

Log Splinter, various editions. USNA Nimitz Library, Special Collections, Annapolis, Md.

Lovette, Leland P., Commander. *School of the Sea.* New York: Frederick A. Stokes, 1941.

Lucky Bag. Annapolis, Md., 1894–date.

Lull, Edward P., Lieutenant Commander. "Description and History of the U.S. Naval Academy From Its Origin to the Present." 1869. USNA Archives, Annapolis, Md.

Mack, William P., Vice Admiral, and Royal W. Connell. *Naval Ceremonies, Customs and Traditions.* Annapolis, Md.: Naval Institute Press, 1980.

Magruder, P. H. "The U.S. Naval Academy and Annapolis during the Civil War 1861–1865." *Proceedings* (USNI), April 1946.

Marshall, Edward Chauncey. *History of the Naval Academy.* New York: D. Van Nostrand, 1862.

McKee, Kinnaird R., Admiral. "Report to the Secretary of Defense on the Pertinence of the U.S. Naval Academy Curriculum to the Officer Needs of the Navy and Marine Corps," June 20, 1978.

Mersky, Peter B., and Norman Polmar. *The Naval Air War in Vietnam.* Annapolis, Md.: Nautical & Aviation Publishing Co. of America, 1981.

Morison, Samuel Eliot. *The Oxford History of the American People.* New York: Oxford University Press, 1965.

Musser, Neil Borgquist. *My Life at the U.S. Naval Academy.* Haldeman-Julius Company, ND.

"Navy Olympic Medal Winners." Condensed from "Navy Men in the Olympic Games." *Proceedings* (USNI), August 1960. Updated by Tom Bates, 1992.

North, Oliver L. *Under Fire: An American Story.* New York: Harper Collins, 1991.

Patrick, K. W. "Midshipman Cruises." *Proceedings* (USNI), October 1935.

Photo Albums. USNA Nimitz Library, Special Collections, Annapolis, Md.

Potter, E. B. *Nimitz.* Annapolis, Md.: Naval Institute Press, 1976.

Prange, Gordon W. *Miracle at Midway.* New York: McGraw-Hill, 1982.

Proceedings, various editions. U.S. Naval Institute, Annapolis, Md.

"Professional Athletes from the Naval Academy." USNA Sports Information chart.

The Publick Enterprise, various editions. Annapolis, Md.

Reef Points, various years. Annapolis, Md.

Register of Alumni. United States Naval Academy Alumni Association, Annapolis, Md., 1991.

Report of the Board of Visitors to the United States Naval Academy, various years. USNA Archives, Annapolis, Md.

Riesenberg, Felix, Jr. *The Story of the Naval Academy.* New York: Random House, 1958.

"Sailing at the Naval Academy." *Proceedings* (USNI), April 1946.

Santoli, Al. *Everything We Had.* New York: Random House, 1981.

Schoor, Gene. *100 Years of Army-Navy Football.* New York: Henry Holt, 1989.

Scrapbooks. USNA Nimitz Library, Special Collections, Annapolis, Md.

Sebald, William J. "Papers of William J. Sebald, 1917–1918." USNA Nimitz Library, Special Collections, Annapolis, Md.

Shipmate, various editions. United States Naval Academy Alumni Association, Annapolis, Md.

Smallwood, William L. *The Naval Academy Candidate Book.* Litchfield Park, Ariz.: Beacon Books, 1989.

Smith, Roy C. III, Captain. "The First Hundred Years Are . . ." *Proceedings* (USNI), October 1973.

Soley, James Russell. "Historical Sketches of the United States Naval Academy." Washington, D.C.: Government Printing Office, 1876.

Spector, Ronald H. *Eagle Against the Sun: The American War with Japan.* New York: Free Press, 1985.

Sturdy, Henry Francis. "The Founding of the Naval Academy by Bancroft and Buchanan." *Proceedings* (USNI), October 1935.

Sweetman, Jack. *The U.S. Naval Academy.* Annapolis, Md.: Naval Institute Press, 1979.

Todorich, Charles. *The Spirited Years.* Annapolis, Md.: Naval Institute Press, 1984.

Trident. Annapolis, Md.: USNA Public Affairs Office, December 7, 1990–date.

Uhlig, Frank, Jr. *Vietnam: The Naval Story.* Annapolis, Md.: Naval Institute Press, 1986.

USNA Catalog, various years. Washington, D.C.: Government Printing Office.

USNA Public Affairs Office. Various press releases and publications.

USNA Sports Information files. Army-Navy; Joe Bellino; Coaches; Individual Sports; Mascots; Napoleon McCallum; David Robinson; Roger Staubach; Team Sports.

USNA Sports Programs. Various sports, various years.

Vertical Files—USNA. USNA Nimitz Library, Special Collections.

Warren, Mame, and Marion E. Warren. *Everybody Works But John Paul Jones*. Annapolis, Md.: Naval Institute Press, 1981.

Webb, James H. *A Sense of Honor*. Englewood Cliffs, N.J.: Prentice-Hall, 1981.

West, Richard S., Jr. "The Superintendents of the Naval Academy." *Proceedings* (USNI), April 1946.

Wilson, Art. *"No Excuses Allowed."* New York: Dead Reckoning Press, 1991.

Wilson, William E., Lieutenant. "Graduates of the U.S. Naval Academy." *Proceedings* (USNI), April 1946.

U.S. Naval Institute Oral History Program, Annapolis, Md.

Reminiscences of:

Hanson Weightman Baldwin

Slade D. Cutter, Captain

John F. Davidson, Rear Admiral

Frederick A. Edwards, Sr., Captain

Francis D. Foley, Rear Admiral

Thomas J. Hamilton, Rear Admiral

Stephen Jurika, Jr., Captain

Draper L. Kauffman, Rear Admiral

Alex A. Kerr, Captain

Mrs. Marc A. Mitscher
    and Mrs. Roy C. Smith, Jr.

William R. Smedberg III, Vice Admiral

John S. Thach, Admiral

Alfred G. Ward, Admiral

Joseph M. Worthington, Rear Admiral

Authors' Interviews and Correspondence

C. H. Barber, Commander.

James Barber, Captain.

Carol Baysinger, USNA Social Director.

William S. Busik, Captain.

James F. Calvert, Vice Admiral.

James Earl Carter, The Honorable.

James W. Cheevers, USNA
    Museum Curator.

Color Girls.

William B. Garrett, USNA
    Vice Academic Dean.

Michael John, Commander.

William P. Lawrence, Vice Admiral.

Jack Lengyel, USNA
    Director of Athletics.

Thomas C. Lynch, Rear Admiral.

William P. Mack, Vice Admiral.

Emmy Marshall, First USNA
    Social Director.

Kinnaird R. McKee, Admiral.

Charles S. Minter, Jr., Vice Admiral.

Thomas H. Moorer, Admiral.

Terrence P. Murray, Colonel.

John L. Prehn, Jr., Captain.

John W. Ripley, Colonel.

Ann Rondeau, Commander.

Paul Stillwell, USNA Graduate,
    Director of History Division,
    U.S. Naval Institute.

USNA Graduates and Midshipmen

Anthony J. Watson, Rear Admiral.

James A. Winnefeld, Rear Admiral.

Photocredits

The Bettman Archive: pages: 79, 81, 82 (bottom), 86–87

Anthony Edgeworth: pages: 1, 8–9, 15, 16–17, 18–19, 23, 26, 30 (bottom left), 32–33, 34–35, 89, 90, 91 (top and bottom), 92 (top and bottom), 93, 95, 104, 120, 121, 123, 126, 129 (top center), 130 (top and bottom), 140 (top), 142, 144 (bottom), 145, 146–147, 172, 192–193

Bob Grieser: pages: 20, 184, 187 (top), 188, 190–191

Phil Hoffman: pages: 132 (bottom), 148, 157, 160, 162 (top and bottom), 163, 165, 166, 169, 171, 174–175, 176, 180, 182–183

Keith Jenkins: pages: 2–3, 4–5, 6–7, 10–11, 12, 24–25, 27, 28 (top and bottom), 29, 30 (top, right and left), 31, 88, 94, 97, 98 (top and bottom), 99, 100 (top and bottom), 102–103, 107, 108, 109, 112 (bottom), 113 (all), 115 (top and bottom), 124–125, 134 (top and bottom), 135 (top and bottom), 138 (top and bottom), 185, 186 (top and bottom), 187 (right), 189, 196–197

USNA Archives: pages: 36, 39, 42, 45, 49, 55, 56, 59, 60–61, 62, 64, 67, 69, 70, 71, 72, 73, 74, 77, 82 (top), 84, 85 (top and bottom), 106, 110, 111, 112 (top), 114, 116, 117, 118, 127, 128 (top and bottom), 129 (right center), 131, 132 (top), 133, 137, 143, 144 (top), 150 (top and bottom), 151 (top and bottom), 152, 153, 155, 158, 159, 164

USNA Museum, Beverly Robinson Collection: pages: 47, 50, 57 (top and bottom)

USNA Nimitz Library Special Collections: page: 52

USNA Photo Lab: pages: 28 (center), 96, 101, 139, 140 (bottom)